Dear Dentists,

Thank you for picking up "TikTok Marketing for Dentists: No Dancing Involved". Over the past 12 years, I've dedicated myself to assisting dentists in growing their practices through the vast realm of the internet. TikTok presents a fresh avenue for you to engage with a novel audience.

At this juncture, I would like to wholeheartedly dedicate this book to Dr Nauvneel Kashyap (Nauv). A little over a decade ago, I embarked on this dental marketing journey when I started working with Nauv, blissfully unaware of where it would lead. To say he is the most astute businessperson I've had the privilege to know would be an understatement. His unwavering trust and the countless opportunities he's presented over the years have been monumental. I deeply value the continued support he's given to both me and my business. Nauv, a heartfelt thank you is in order.

Should any part of this book leave you with questions or if you simply wish to delve deeper into the intricacies of marketing, please scan the QR code below to schedule a call with me directly.
Once more, thank you for choosing this book. I sincerely hope it brings value to your practice.

Warm regards,

Josh Rimmington

Josh Rimmington

Scan the QR Code below to book a call with Josh

DEDICATION

In loving memory of my Mami and Mrs. J

To all the women: Breath! Don't forget to laugh in this journey called life.

When you feel overwhelmed, tired, and lonely, play Yolanda Adams, "Still I Rise." The voice within will speak to you

---

PREFACE

I n this humorous but realistic insight about women,
I share how simple yet complex we are. Let's be
honest: Women can be a challenge to understand.
Even among ourselves at times, we are peculiar beings.
We demand it all- career, love, children, and more- and
most times, we deserve it. After all, we carry the weight
of the world on our shoulders and sacrifice so much.
Surprisingly, it is the small things we forget to do, like
laugh. I'm not talking about that little giggle thing we do
trying to look cute. I'm referring to the kind of laughter
you feel in the pit of your gut, and it feels like you've
been doing sit-ups all day. What a joyous (and painful!)
feeling. Do you still have that kind of laugh? Or are you
caught up in the things you demand but have yet to have
or experience?

I know, disappointment is no laughing matter. As women, we are the ones who feel obligated to smile when everyone else can express their vulnerabilities and pain without reprimand. But we can control this mindset. The first thing we need to understand is that we are not perfect Ladies, beating ourselves up evokes no remedy or relief. We must not take ourselves so seriously and learn to laugh with humility. We are imperfectly perfect! Embrace It. Love It.

He's got a job we're moving

"Oh, just sit still," Whitney tells me as I fidget uncomfortably in a chair in her living room, trying to look natural, as I smile at the camera she is holding "I hate this," I say through gritted teeth. I may have hated sitting for a photograph, but I wanted Whitney to take a picture of me for a long time now. She is a natural and has an eye for capturing the beauty in any person or piece. Besides, nice photographs of me are few and far between, so I was past due for a great photo. I was beginning to feel guilty using those filters from my camera phone all the time. "I know, but it's going to look great," Whitney reassures me.

Whitney lives down the street from me. She is friendly and creative. She has a love for art and creativity that is felt in her presence. Even her home replicates her

IMPERFECTLY PERFECT

personality-free. Her house walls are decorated with many photographs she's taken over the years, along with paintings by artists like Kara Walker and Barkley L. Hendricks. There isn't a time when I visit her that I am not fascinated by at least one of her photos.

"That picture is beautiful," I say, noticing a photo on the mantle and finally getting in the perfect position for Whitney to take my picture.

"That's good. Hold it right there. Okay, smile."

Click. "Got it," Whitney says, appearing satisfied.

I forward my attention back to the photo. It was a black and white photograph she'd taken of her mother.

"The shadows..." I let out a short whistle. "If I could take pictures like that, I'd be working for some art magazine or something."

She shrugs and then scrunches up her pretty features. "Don't get me started," she says softly.

I look at her. "What do you mean?"

She shakes her head and waves her hand as if to dismiss her thoughts. "It's just one of those days. They happen every once in a while."

One of those days?" I ask, arching my eyebrow, gesturing the request for an explanation.

***

CARMEN ASHE

Whitney sighs. "You know that Monica song, "For You I Will?"

***

"Sure," I say, vaguely remembering the song. I can hear tiny parts of it in my head, and I'm trying to recall at least the hook. However, the other Monica song comes to mind. "Don't Take It Personal (Just One of Dem Days)" and confuses me a little.

***

She starts to hum the tune, and then she softly sings:

"I will cross the ocean for you

I will go and bring you the moon

I will be your hero, your strength, anything you need

I will be the sun in your sky

I will light your way for all time,

I promise you

For you, I will."

I find it interesting that she chooses that song to describe how she feels.

"I guess I'm just tired of being everyone's everything, you know? I have to be the hero, the sun, and the moon. Even the sun gets a break at night," she says somewhat hopelessly.

I frown, and my expression displays empathy. We walk to the kitchen and sit down at the table where two steaming cups of coffee await us.

"Sounds sad," I offer, not sure exactly what to say but understanding her feelings.

She smiles her regular, warm smile. "I don't mean it to be sad," she replies quickly. "I just don't get why it's always us who have to make all the compromises."

"I know what you mean, but somebody has to do it. And you know if it were up to the men, it wouldn't be done right. Sorry to say."

"Gurl," she says, bringing her cup of coffee to her lips. "You ain't lying about that."

Oh, I thought, this is going to be an interesting photo session!

I lean back in my chair and consider what she said. I didn't disagree at all, not even for a second. Why doesn't a woman compromise when it comes to making things work in a relationship? I quickly reflect on the years of my marriage and the various relationships my friends had. I find myself hard-pressed to come up with more than a handful of times when the men in our lives made genuine concessions to make the relationships work. I know, I know - I can already hear all the men complaining: "What are you talking about?" But seriously, what compromises or sacrifices have most men made? They think they're compromising or doing us the biggest favor by remembering to put the toilet seat down! Yet, some of them miss the toilet entirely.

Still, it seems a curious time to bring the subject up.

"Are things all right between you and Mike?" I ask cautiously.

She rolls her eyes and waves away the concern. "Sure. Fine as always," she says, unconvincingly, probably not believing it herself.

I give her my 'Now-you-know-me-better-than-that look.'

"No - it's nothing," she explains. "Every once in a while, I have a day like this. You know, a couple of loads of wash too many. One of the kids complaining about homework. The weather - who knows?" she says, a bit regretfully, looking down to the floor.

She continues, "I think of what might have been if Mike never got that offer." She exhales deeply and sips her coffee.

***

I knew a little of their history: How they met as students and had fallen in love. They were living in New York City after graduation. Whitney was working as an intern for a fashion photographer. She'd also been doing some work as a stylist, hoping to work for a fashion magazine. Her plans were thrown into disarray when Mike was given a great job offer too good to refuse.

In one of our earliest conversations, Whitney told me, "We decided to get married, move out of state, and start our perfect family." That - Whitney would later tell me - was the "watered-down version."

I knew exactly what she meant. We all had those "tidied-up" versions of our lives, the ones we advertise and share with certain people. I was aware of this version that glosses over the difficult times - the shouting, the hurt, the betrayals. We all offer the version that only depicts our relationships as perfect and happy, our children as wonderful and darling, and our home life as joyous and stable.

"We all want our lives to be like our senior picture in high school," she states with a cynical smile. "All the pimples filtered—an elegant pose, full of youth and promise. We want our lives to look like there's still so much left in us to do more, be more. I suppose that's one reason why I like photography. You can manipulate what people see in the photo while still hiding reality. But in real life, it's not so simple. We can't make the blemishes fade away."

I see what she means, but I can't ignore that she has a nice life with Mike. They have two adorable and obedient children and a lovely home. Plus, Mike has a good job.

"I know, girl, but when you sit and really think about it, you have a decent, good life," I say with encouragement.

"Except for the times I think I might lose my mind," Whitney says with a laugh.

Who hasn't felt like that?

Whitney and Mike had come a long way. Mike studied business, and Whitney studied art in college. She even had an exhibit of her photos at a student show. They had lived together in the West Village. During the summer before her senior year, she had interned at a fashion magazine.

"Loved it," she told me a while ago when we first met.

At first, she had been little more than a gofer - folding clothes, getting coffee, whatever needed to be done. But at one fashion shoot, she'd gotten the courage to ask a question about lighting and f-stops and soon was having a very involved conversation with the photographer.

After that, she was more than just a gofer. She worked exclusively on the shoots.

At the same time, with graduation looming, her relationship with Mike had become more serious. They were both about to face the future, and they wanted to do it together.

Mike's internship had earned him a job offer out of state. Whitney's earned her a chance to work at the magazine.

They married and moved out of state.

***

"You can still take pictures," I tell her supportively.

She makes a face. "I haven't taken my camera out for years," she says. "I'm only taking your picture because you're a good friend," she admits. "Besides, so much has changed in photography." She pauses then shrugs her shoulder. "Oh well, this too shall pass."

"What do you think would have happened if you stayed in New York and worked for that magazine?" I wonder out loud.

"Who knows?" she responds, her eyes drifting out of space in curiosity.

Who did know? Maybe she'd be a famous photographer; maybe she'd be a working mom in New York. Or perhaps her life path would have brought her somehow to this very same house and neighborhood.

Maybe Mike would have worked on Wall Street or in a neighborhood bank. Or maybe he would have been the financial manager for a manufacturing plant.

We never know what life holds or what life would have held. However, I know that for women - when it is a choice between his job or hers; between staying put or chasing a dream; between keeping her career or leaving with him - there isn't much of a choice at all.

Oh, and as for Monica putting women on the spot to be on-call super-she-ros, Miss Thang is on time-out!

CHAPTER 2

Stand by your man; that's the dumbest idea ever

"You want to do what?" Lord, what gets into a man's head for him to think that any idea that pops in his head can be turned into a genuine, money-making enterprise? Janet thinks to herself. She turns her attention from the dishes she was finishing, wipes her hands on the dishtowel, and then faces her husband, Kenny, seated at the kitchen table. More likely, she was thinking of a lot more, most of which should not find its way into print!

Have you lost your mind? was one of the milder questions that almost makes its way past her lips. Although she could not have been more frustrated, she tries to hold her tongue and see things from his perspective. However, her mind is on replaying the scene in Poetic Justice when Janet Jackson is in the store, and Tammy Wynette's "Stand by Your Man" is playing. (Depending on where you are in your relationship, you either love the song or hate it.) .

Janet's man, Kenny, was beaten up and depressed. Kenny had lost his position at a trucking company several months earlier and, after a couple of construction jobs and a few odd jobs ended, hadn't had much to do with his time except "strategize," as he called it.

Okay, Janet understood that Kenny's ego had taken a bruising. She also got that he didn't like that only her salary as a nurse kept them afloat. "Suck it up," she had wanted to tell him. "Bag groceries. Mow lawns. Do something!" But she didn't. She kept her feelings to herself. She knew what it meant to walk on eggshells around his tender yet masculine ego. She, like most of us girls and women, learned that lesson very early in life. The bruised male psyche is nothing to trifle with. The distance between the man you married and a five-year-old is not nearly as far as you might have suspected it would be when you stood next to him, handsome in his tux, at the altar.

So, Kenny was in a funk. Join the club, Janet figured. Life's tough sometimes. It's not like jobs are going to come knocking on the door. And if you don't feel like going out looking for work, would it be so terrible to do a little more around the house or helping with the girls? Apparently not. What he was doing more and more was "strategizing" — an activity which, seeing it from Janet's perspective, looked more and more like watching stupid television programs from the couch.

A load of wash would have been nice. Even just cleaning up after himself or wiping the bathroom. And while he was at it, couldn't he wear something other than that raggedy Captain America tee-shirt? At least let her run it through the wash?

What grown man gets so attached to a tee-shirt? She didn't care that the first movie he went to see was Captain America. The shirt needed washing.

Hell, it needed throwing away. It was so threadbare you could almost see through it.

Still, she had to give credit where credit was due. He was putting forth more than a fair amount of effort, thinking about what he could do to get back on his feet. Of course, I'd like him to do more than just think about what he could do, she mused more than once.

Yes, she wanted him to do something other than just think of a plan. She already knew he had no problem thinking of a plan. He could think all day- sit his Captain America Tee-shirt-wearing, fake-strategizing, non-laundry-doing ass on the couch and make that brain work like he was Einstein or somebody. What Kenny failed to do is think of a good plan. Perhaps, Janet was downplaying his efforts. At least he had ambitions, right?

Janet was more logical than most people. She believed that plans needed to be methodical and assessed from every possible direction. At times, she wondered if she applied the concept to choosing who she'd marry.

"A pet grooming service?" she stammers, unable to hide the exasperation from her voice. Her face is flush red and not just from the hot water she used to rinse the dishes.

"It's perfect," he says, cheerfully oblivious to her frustration. "Who doesn't need their pets groomed?" he goes on, as though the logic behind his reasoning was so obvious that it hardly needed stating. "And no one likes to do it themselves."

"Yes, every pet needs grooming," Janet reasons, not finding the leap between the fact that every pet needed grooming and the fact that Kenny wasn't doing a particularly good job of grooming himself lately an easy one to make. Let's not forget the Captain America shirt. "What does that have to do with you becoming a pet groomer? What are you going to do? Polish Fifi's toenails?"

He looks at her like she is crazy or trying to be funny. His expression practically shouts: Of course, woman! Stop playing. You already know!

"Oh, Kenny," she cries out, her voice filled with the frustration and exasperation that she knew, on reflection, must have sounded like his mother to him. "What the hell do you know about grooming pets?"

"I give Dash a bath," he defends, trying not very well to hide the hurt in his voice.

"You have not given Dash a bath," she says firmly, thinking about their pet mutt. "You've hosed him down a couple of times - not the same thing." .

He is silent, clearly hurt by her reaction. He was crazy. He was making weird, ridiculous plans that she was sure would cost them a lot more money than they would possibly make, and yet she was the one feeling guilty. What's wrong with this picture, she wonders to herself. Why did she feel terrible because Kenny was acting ridiculous?

But she did.

She offers a sad, sympathetic face. "Kenny, I don't know if this is the way to go with this."

His eyes flash with hurt and anger. To Janet, his whole-body language screams, 'I can't stand you. You're such a miserable person. You're just like your mother!'

She knows he means, "You're just like my mother!" but she does not think this was the time to make the correction. If he doesn't know my mom from his mom, that's another issue, Janet says in her head.

While his body language said one thing, this is what he actually said: "You're just negative. You've always been negative. I can't stand you!" he squints his eyes at her in disgust. "For your information, I've done some research."

She didn't know it, but he'd actually gone into local pet stores and spoken to the store owners about his plans. They were encouraging enough. Why not? Sure, they'd put out his "business card" and sell him all the grooming supplies he needed.

"Did you know you need surgical grade scissors to trim a dog's nails?" he states, trying to sound credible and prove the point that he knew what he was talking about.

"Kenny... KENNY..."

Kenny stares at her. He could see that, despite her efforts to be calm and rational, she is upset. He could tell from the way she picks at her cuticles like she always did when she was upset.

"What? What's the matter? Why can't you ever be positive about anything I want to do?"

With that, he gets up and storms out of the house.

Janet feels a chill go through her. How many times had Kenny made some stupid decision that set back their finances for months, if not years? How many stupid decisions had he made that meant the kids couldn't take dance lessons? Or music lessons? Or participate in an afternoon basketball game?

This was another stupid decision- a foolish one. Janet knew with every fiber of her being that it was the wrong decision. But she also knew that she would not oppose Kenny going forward.

She just felt so bad when she didn't let him get his way. It was almost as though she was afraid and reluctant to tell him the truth. Deep down, she resented how he was supposed to be the protector, yet she was the one always trying to protect his feelings or protect their family from his irrational decisions.

She internalizes his anger and his words, using them against herself, getting herself off balance. "Am I negative? Haven't I been supportive?"

And what would happen if she didn't go along with his crazy plan? She shuddered to think about it.

***

"Are you crazy?" Michelle, Janet's best friend, asks when she tells her about Kenny's plan and her going along. "What are you thinking?"

Janet couldn't say it out loud, but she knows exactly what she is thinking. She thinks if she pushes too hard, if she disagrees with Kenny, if she doesn't support him so that he believes she's in his corner, then he would leave her.

As hard as it might be to deal with the financial hardship, his leaving was more than she was willing to put up with. In her mind, it was better to be wrong, to be foolish, to be walked all over, than to be alone.

After all, she learned to dance without formal lessons.

And Kenny did look awfully cute in that Captain America tee shirt, and "Stand by Your Man" was one of the best-selling hit singles by a female in the history of country music.

Who knows? Maybe one day, Kenny will conjure a plan that sets them up for life. For now, she needed to go online and see if she could find some surgical-grade scissors.

CHAPTER 3

Do I look like an ATM?

S hirley could almost hear in her mind's eye how the conversation must have gone: "Hey, babe. Do you have any extra money? I just have to cover my rent until I get paid for this wiring job I'm working on." The thought of it made Shirley want to slap some sense into both of them.

***

Faith, Shirley's twenty-three-year-old daughter, would have smiled as she held the phone to her ear, loving the sound of his voice. Shirley hated Chris. He was bad, bad, bad, bad. She only wished that she didn't know what her daughter saw in him. But she did. She'd been twenty-three once. It had been almost a week since Faith had heard from him, and she felt like she was going through withdrawal.

18 | Page

"How much do you need?" Faith had replied.

Not a tremble in her voice. Not a moment of doubt. If you were to have a medical device that allowed you to look into Faith's mind, you would have been able to visualize pure joy. That's right, pure joy!

It's not that Faith liked being a human ATM. And it's not that Faith was a trust fund baby, sitting on a pile of money that she just loved to give away. Shirley had taught her the need to be smart about her money, to put away something for that rainy day.

***

Faith was not a foolish girl. Although she was young, she'd been working since she'd been in high school, waiting tables, scooping ice cream, baby-sitting. Now, thanks to a friend of Shirley's, she had a decent job as a secretary in an insurance office. Faith knew that she would never get rich on her salary, but she could afford her apartment, her car payments, and her student loan payments so she could continue to take classes in the evening. She got health care through work. And she liked the people she worked with. Faith was pretty much handling her business.

She was a busy girl; between work and school, she had very little downtime. As a result, she had been feeling a bit lonely. That is until she and some girlfriends had gone out for a "girls' night" to drink, dance, and play a little pool.

That night, she had met Chris. From where she sat with her girlfriends, huddled together over a single stool by the bar, he was Jason Momoa in blue jeans – muscle-clenching tee-shirt, hair a bit mussed and longer than she usually liked. Still, there was something about him. He did appear rather rough around the edges, but she could not deny that she was attracted to him.

He'd caught her eye. The next thing she knew, he was coming over to ask her to dance. Well, the rest of the night was anything but "girls' night." Dancing, drinking, sloppy kissing.

"Where have you been all my life?" he had asked her as her girlfriends tugged her out of the bar to go home.

"The question is," she'd said with a killer smile, "where will I be the rest of your life?"

With that, she'd taken his phone, added her name to his Contacts, and then allowed herself to be dragged, giggling and happy, off into the night.

It seemed to be a perfect, magical night. She had really enjoyed herself and was also proud of herself. She hadn't done anything "stupid." There was a time when she may have, but that evening, she had allowed her girlfriends to pull her away- a perk of going to the club with your girls.

The following morning, she had awakened in her own bed with nothing but a very dull and distant headache to cloud her happiness at such an enjoyable evening. Had she expected Chris to call? She couldn't say. But when he had, she could not help but smile.

"Hey," he had said. "I bet you don't know who this is."

"Oh, no?" she'd teased. "And what's it worth to me if I do know?"

He laughed. "Dinner and a movie."

"Hmm. There's a lot on the line then, isn't there? Do I get three guesses?"

There had been something about Chris that swept her off her feet. He was rugged, charming, and sweet that first date and the next couple. He was so different than the young men in the office where she worked or the students at school. She had enjoyed his company. Faith had not thought anything of paying for one of their dinners. It wasn't like she was one of those snowflake girls who had to have a boy hold the door open for her. She was working. She liked the idea of equality.

It had not been that Chris was spending nights with her at her apartment. Even so, she could tell he couldn't be easily "tamed." He had a rough restlessness about him. Shirley had cautioned her to take things slow.

"Don't get yourself into something you can't get out of," Shirley had advised, listening suspiciously to her daughter going on and on about how special Chris was.

She had never dated anyone like him before. She felt alive when she was with him. It wasn't like he was trying to trick her. He had been candid about his job situation. He'd patched together his income from construction work and odd bartending jobs on the weekend. Although he had been a few years older than Faith, he managed to live his life like a college student.

Faith had found that somehow admirable.

***

"He's a bum," Shirley had said during a talk with her daughter.

"Mom! He works. He just doesn't work like you want him to."

"What does he want to do with his life?" Shirley insisted, questionably.

Faith had heard her mother talking, but she wasn't listening, and she certainly wasn't going to take heed. What's all that go to do with me, Faith had thought, rolling her eyes.

None of that mattered to her. She felt herself falling in love with Chris. Sometimes he would call in the middle of the week and ask if she wanted to go out dancing. Other times, he didn't call for a week or more. As the days went by without her hearing from him, she'd felt her heart grow heavy. She had become more distracted at work, and her friends grew concerned. A couple of times, they had tried to convince her to come out for a "girls' night," but she usually had an excuse for not being able to go.

"You saw how that worked out last time," she had responded sarcastically, referring to the night she met Chris.

"That's different," one of Faith's friends had said. "That boy got you sprung, girl," she'd teased.

Faith had shaken her head. "It's not even like that, and I am not sprung."

Her friend had kept going. "Okay, so you telling me you don't check your phone or wait for him to call?"

Whatever Faith had thought. *At least I got a man.* She wasn't going to admit that maybe she did anticipate hearing from him. Sometimes, it had been the highlight of her day. When he did call, it was as if the sun miraculously burst through heavy storm clouds. Flowers bloomed. Angels sang.

That day, the phone rang while Faith had been folding some laundry at home. The sound startled her, and she immediately looked at her phone. It was from Chris. Her heart melted and pounded at the same time.

He offered his usual greeting.

"Hey. Sorry, it's been a while. It's been crazy busy on this construction job."

Had she berated him for his inconsideration? Had she said how hurt she felt? No. Not a peep. Just: "Hey, yourself. How've you been?"

They had chatted briefly, and then Chris asked for some money. Faith did not hesitate or ask what he needed the money for. She did not factor in that her rent was due, and she still had to stretch her own paycheck.

"No problem," she'd said when he said that if she couldn't do it, he'd figure something else out.

She just kept smiling, happy to have him on the phone. But happier and damn-near honored to be the one who could help him in his time of need.

"When do you want to come by to pick it up?" she'd asked, making a mental note at the same time that as soon as she got off the phone with Chris, she would have to phone her mother.

She would have to borrow some money to make her rent.

It was not uncommon for Faith to ask Shirley for money. And Shirley always tried to help. She was proud of her daughter and how she was making her way in the world. She knew that an unexpected bill, car trouble, needing books - anything could throw off a young woman on a tight budget.

I could tell something was going on, Shirley thought, her inner voice filled with hesitation and anger. Faith didn't sound like herself when she asked for some money. So, I asked her if everything was all right. I got the usual, "everything's fine, mom" stuff. Well, I wasn't interested in that.

After a bit more poking, Faith confessed the real reason that she asked for money.

"Oh, honey," Shirley said, unable to hide the frustration in her voice. "I want you to listen to "Heartbreak Hotel" by Whitney Houston.

You're making a big mistake."

"Mom, please. Just help me out this once."

Of course, Shirley helped her out. With the full knowledge that "this once" could easily be many more times. Faith was on a path to learn one of the lessons that women have been learning for thousands of years. We always seem to be willing to break the bank for our man, no matter how foolish we're being.

***

When's the last time a man took out a second-mortgage because his wife or girlfriend asked him "pretty please" for some money?

***

Ladies, what do we think when we turn ourselves into personal ATMs for our men? When the genders are reversed, women are called gold-diggers. In some cases, when certain activities are involved, we can also be known as other unmentionable terms. But what's the word used to describe a man who uses a woman for money and has nothing going for himself? Oh, yeah, there's scrub, bum, deadbeat - more than I thought, actually. Still, when did it become okay for men to depend on women financially? Maybe I'm old-school, but it doesn't sit right with me. And I'm not saying I'm some kind of feminist, but I think a man should have his own backbone. Everyone needs help sometimes, but some of you men need to get it together. Where is the pride, my brothers?

I can't help but remember when I was a little girl, and I wanted something my parents wouldn't buy for me. My mom would tell me, "money doesn't grow on trees." She was right. Apparently, we just print it up ourselves sometimes! And good men don't just fall out of the sky and end up at nightclubs.

That evening Faith came by to pick up the money, and Shirley was purposely playing on repeat Heartbreak Hotel by Whitney Houston.

CHAPTER 4

What am I going to wear?

It doesn't matter if you're sixteen or forty-six; there's nothing like a first date to get the butterflies fluttering in your stomach.

After nineteen years of marriage and two kids, my friend Gladys had been divorced for almost a year. For most of that time, she had sworn to herself, No Men! It wasn't just the divorce, but the long, difficult and exhausting struggle getting to the divorce. She couldn't believe that the man she had once been married to, the man she had once been in love with, could be so difficult about everything.

"It wasn't like we fought a lot. We just fell out of love, I guess," she explained with a sigh. "1 don't blame him. I don't know why he has to blame me."

Like marriages, divorces are tricky.

"The last thing I was interested in was getting into another relationship. Since my divorce, the only song I played constantly was Carole King's "It's too late."

But sleeping in a big bed by yourself has a way of making you think that maybe being "out there" isn't such a crazy thing after all.

But who would have us? We may feel like we're sixteen but we're sure not sixteen anymore. No more tight, flat bellies for us! It doesn't matter if you work out ten hours a week or do yoga or run marathons. You're not getting that "before babies" body back.

No, our bodies somehow manage to betray every experience we've gone through, from the lines on our faces to our strong hips. No new moisturizers or undergarments can get rid of the years.

Which can make "dating" a pretty strange experience when you get to be of a certain age. Men our own ages all want young women, and we aren't really interested in shopping around for older men who mostly want someone to take care of them, some combination of a sister and a mother.

So, it was quite a shock when — what felt like out of nowhere — Eddie asked her out. Gladys worked in a good-sized office. There was consensus among the women working there that, without question, Eddie was the most available and interesting man at work. Tall. In good shape. He had a love for long runs on the weekends and considerate gestures at work. He never forgot to wish a coworker a happy birthday. If he asked you how your day was, he made you feel that he was really interested in the answer.

He was always polite. Always charming.

"Who do you think he's dating?" ."He's got to be dating someone."

"You don't think he's gay, do you?"

"He can't be married. He doesn't have a ring on his finger. My friend in HR

said he wasn't 't married."

"Oh, please don't tell me he lives with his mother!"

"I think that's cute."

"Shut up!"

The gossip about Eddie was a secret vice of most of the women in the office, whether they were single or married, young or old. His kindness and quick smile just melted every woman's heart. Gladys wasn't much of a gossiper, but she'd overheard the others. She didn't gossip, but she didn't disagree. Eddie was a really nice guy — the kind of guy that the women agreed was few and far between. Still, even though he would smile and say hello to her when they passed in the halls, she sometimes wondered if he actually knew who she was.

Then, during a staff meeting, Gladys happened to mention that she was going on a day hike the following weekend. Eddie seemed to perk up a bit.

"Where do you hike?" he asked.

"I'm sorry?"

"Where do you hike?" he asked.

She said that there was a place about an hour north of the city with some really beautiful trails. He nodded. "Sure," he said. "I know them well. I like to go up there and run those trails."

She laughed softly before trying to turn her attention back to the meeting. "I'm happy to walk them," she said.

"Well," he conceded with a smile. "Walking's good. Maybe we could walk them sometime."

"That would be great," she said.

After the meeting, Shania, another junior accountant, nudged Gladys. "He was flirting with you," she said.

Gladys made a face. "No, he wasn't."

Shania gave her a knowing look. "Yes, he was."

Gladys just waved her off, but the idea had been planted in her imagination that he was, and she could not deny that the idea that he would flirt with her made her walk just a bit lighter on her feet.

After that, whenever Gladys would pass Eddie in the hall, he seemed to hold her gaze a bit longer than he had. Then, on Friday afternoon, he asked her if she would like to have dinner and go to a movie Saturday evening, "Unless you're going to be away hiking or something," he said with a quick, easy smile.

"Play it cool! Play it cool!" Gladys told herself. She took a slow breath. "That sounds nice," she said. "I'd like that."

"Great. About 7:30?"

"Perfect." She gave him her phone number and address and then pretty much floated through the remainder of the day. She didn't see Eddie the following day which was, in her mind, just as well. She was sure that she'd say or do something ridiculous.

"It's just dinner and a movie," she told Shania, who was not at all convinced that her nonchalance demeanor was sincere.

"Just dinner and a movie?! It's a date, you silly girl! You're going out on a date with Mr. Wonderful himself." Gladys laughed.

"You better call me and spill all the details on Sunday morning," Shania told her. "Unless, of course, the date is still going on," she teased.

"Oh, stop..." Gladys said, her cheeks reddening.

It was ridiculous that Shania was so excited about the date. It was just dinner and a movie between office colleagues, right?

Still, she couldn't deny that she was excited too. She struggled to remain focused on work for the remainder of the day. On Saturday, without the distraction of work, she was filled with all kinds of emotions. She couldn't believe he'd actually asked her out. (He had, hadn't he? She hadn't dreamt it, had she?)

The theoretical gave way to the practical as the morning turned to early afternoon. What should she wear? Business-like would send the wrong message. So, would something too flirty. Did she even own something flirty? Maybe she should go to the mall and buy something new'?

After going through just about every outfit in her closet, she didn't have time to go to the mall — despite not liking anything she owned. She would just have to make do, which she did by mixing a lovely spring skirt with a white, sleeveless blouse. The kids were at their father's this weekend, and she took full advantage of her alone time. Blasting Shania Twain's "Man I feel like a Woman" as she prepared for her date, After she showered, she put on her robe and did her make-up. Then she went to get dressed. Looking in the mirror, she appraised herself. She didn't like what she saw. In a panic, she called her sister.

"I'm wearing old lady panties!" she whined.

Her sister laughed. "He's not going to see your underwear, or is he?" she said.

"But I look like mom," Gladys sighed.

That stopped her sister short. Unless your mother is a beauty queen, looking in the mirror and seeing your mother is a shock. "You're not mom," she said softly. "Just relax and have a good time. You deserve it."

Not convinced, Gladys was a little calmer as she finished dressing.

She was ready at 7:00.

At 7:15, she was already getting anxious. Maybe he wasn't coming.

At 7:28, she wondered where he was.

At 7:33, she was in a panic, sure she was going to be stood up, maybe he'd tried to call her cell, but the battery was dead or something. She examined her phone. It seemed to be fully charged.

7:35. She was pacing. She was perspiring. If she kept this up, she would have to change again.

7:40. A knock on the door. Now her heart really started to pound. She opened the door. "Hi," she said,

He smiled that smile. "Sorry, I'm a bit late. There was a lot more traffic than I'd expected." "Oh, no problem at all," she said, grabbing her purse and stepping out the door. "I didn't even notice."

CHAPTER 5

Then make a peanut butter and jelly sandwich for dinner!

I get that we women are nurturing by nature. There's a reason that we're the mommies, and that's not to cast any aspersions on any "house-dads". They're great. But they are the exception that proves the rule. Men just can't manage for themselves.

How many times have I heard, "Where's the butter?" shouted by my husband as he stuck his head inside the refrigerator?

I'm sure he was never pleased with my time-worn response, "What do you want it to do, jump out and kiss you?" But I was even more sure that he liked the fact that I came over and immediately found the butter — or that it was right in front of his nose!

Men are, when all is said and done, incapable of taking care of themselves. I'm not suggesting that this weakness (and it is a weakness!) is genetic. I am sure that with the proper training, men could manage just fine. After all, it takes years of focused effort, but I am told that there are several men who have managed to learn to actually put their dilly socks in the hamper and to put down the toilet seat.

There's hope!

But the truth is, when it comes to training our men, it is not the men who are the "enemy." Ladies, let's be honest here, WE are the enemy. Rather than put in the time and energy required to properly train our men, the tables have been turned on us. We are the ones who have been trained.

What I mean by that is simple. Rather than train our men to be self-sufficient, we have been trained to cater to their every whim. This starts at a very young age, from the first time we learned to play "house." Oh sure, we thought the mommy was in charge, but the truth of the matter was a bit more complicated.

Angela almost smacked her forehead in frustration when we were talking about this very thing the other day.

"You're right," she said, her eyes widening in shock. "How many times have my kids been sitting in front of the television and asked for a snack? Did I say to them, 'Get up and get it?' No! That would have been the right thing to do. But I wanted to be the loving, nurturing mommy...so I prepared a snack for them and delivered it to them." She shook her head. "How stupid!"

"You're not being stupid," I told her. "You're being a good mom."

She laughed. "That's what I thought too. But now I realize what I've gotten myself into, what we've all gotten ourselves into."

She went on to describe a "girls' night out" a couple of weeks earlier. She and three of her friends had been having a wonderful time. They'd gone out to a matinee and then dinner. One of her friends suggested that they stop and have a drink, "just to end a great day in a perfect way." As they walked across Broadway singing off-tune, "That's what friends are for." They were all in agreement...until Angela happened to glance at her watch. Realizing the time, she said she wasn't sure if she could.

"What do you mean, if you can?" Stephanie asked. "Do you have a curfew or something?" They all laughed, remembering their high school days when they did have a curfew.

Angela didn't say anything. She slipped away from the group and took her cell from her purse. She quickly called home.

"Hello?"

"Hey, Stevie. It's me,"

"Hey, when are you going to be home? I'm getting hungry.„

She felt a wave of guilt wash over her. That's why she was calling; to find out what he wanted for dinner. "I'll be home soon," she said before putting her cell away.

She felt a flash of anger throughout her body as she apologized for not being able to join them for a drink, but she had to get home to make dinner for Stevie.

"Why did I have to do that?" she asked me, her expression betraying both amusement and frustration. "Why couldn't he fix himself something for dinner, even if it was a bowl of cereal? I mean, my Lord, the man can't even open a can or boil water himself."

I smiled. I knew exactly how Angela felt. I've come home from things a thousand times in a rush just to get dinner ready. I have called ahead more times than I can remember just to ask, what do you want me to make for you?

When I finally arrived home, Stevie was in his recliner watching Football, Basketball, or some stupid sport event. I smiled politely and went straight to the kitchen to prepare his dinner. I was listening to Karyn White's Superwoman. This song has always moved me, but tonight it had a special meaning. I walked him over his dinner, A peanut butter and jelly sandwich. I didn't wait for any response.

I think it's time for some training! *For us*!

CHAPTER 6

He cheated; it's my fault

I don't care if you're a stay-at-home mom, an attorney, or a professional dancer. Nothing cuts as deeply as having your man cheat on you. The hurt is sharp, and then, even if you think you're completely over it, it still throbs like an ache that lets you know a rainstorm is coming.

When a man cheats on his woman, he is an ass. There's no other way to say it, no sense in mincing words. (I could use other choice words, but I'll keep it clean for the sake of this book.) It's just heartbreaking when a man hurts his woman that way. What's even more painful than the cheating is how we turn the hurt inward. We start to blame ourselves like we did something wrong.

Let me tell you about my friend Donna. I met her our sophomore year in high school. She was beautiful and smart - the "It Girl." All the boys wanted her, but she was strictly about her academics. If you were a boy coming to talk to her and the conversation wasn't about school or self-development, she would not pay you any attention. She was determined to make it out of the hood, even if it meant not fitting in or being a part of the crowd.

Donna was different than most of my friends. Whenever my friends and I would gather, we would listen to music, gossip, compare our favorite artists.

"At least Cardi B. admits her body is fake."

"Who cares? Nikki is better at rapping."

"Did you see Beyonce's new video?"

Donna would always find a reason not to hang out with us. I started to wonder if maybe she thought she was better than us in some way because we weren't as focused or driven. When I would ask her why she rarely hung out with us, her response was always the same. "Girl, I have no time for those conversations. Y'all ain't talkin' about nothing that's going to get me into college. I'm trying to get into Howard University on a full Scholarship. Beyonce is not going to buy my books."

I always admired Donna. She knew at 15 what she wanted. Meanwhile, I didn't know what I wanted to do the next day.

Donna got accepted into Howard University on a full scholarship. She was on her path to becoming a lawyer, focused on breaking the cycle of the adults she'd known who had missed their potential. Donna was raised in a single-parent home and had witnessed how difficult it was for her mother. Her dad left when she was six, and throughout the years, she would see him from time to time. Once, she told me that he was more like a distant family member that you would see every couple of years than like a father. Whenever he showed up, she was cordial, polite, and respectful. She never understood why her mother was so nice to him and would let him spend the night.

Donna called me one Saturday afternoon to talk to me about some guy she met in "Chocolate City."

"Chocolate City," I repeated, amused that she was using the term like a native of the area.

"Yes, that's what they call D.C.," Donna schooled me.

I laughed to myself, thinking my friend is trying to get some swag. Two and half hours later, I knew all about Eric. It was interesting to hear her talk about a guy this way since she was not into boys in high school. She was actually quite naive when it came to relationships, unlike myself, who was more experienced. Therefore, I could recognize any warning signs. I listened as a friend, but I knew that Eric was a bad boy from our first conversation. Three years later, accompanied by several "mistakes," Donna found herself pregnant and with an on-again, off-again live-in boyfriend. She told me about his commitment and monogamy problems and how disgustingly forgiving she had become with Eric's drama and disrespect. She had turned into her mother.

One day as Donna passed a mirror, she stopped and stared at her reflection, but instead of seeing herself, she saw her mother. The tears fell immediately like a broken water pipe. They poured down her face uncontrollably. She thought to herself, what's wrong with me? Am I not smart enough, pretty enough? I did everything right. I stayed focus. Am I not enough? She gathered herself together while a string of very impulsive thoughts filled her mind.

Do I throw his clothes out?

Set his car on fire?

Show up at his new girlfriend's house?

Or do I act like my mother and be grateful when he does finally come over? None were an option. Instead, she searched her playlist for Beyonce. She remembered how much Whitney's music inspired her mother and how much Beyonce inspired her.

"OMG!! I have become my mother." She connected her iPhone to her Bose Speaker and blasted "Irreplaceable."

Donna dumped Eric, had a beautiful baby girl named Erica, graduated a semester behind with honors, and is currently working at a prestigious law firm in Washington D.C. Eric attempted several times to play dad with no consistency, and Donna refused to expose her daughter to those emotional scars she experienced as a child. Although she loved, admired, and respected her mom, she would have preferred an absentee father to the one she had.

***

Now, I do not pretend to understand men. If I did, I would be writing a completely different book than I'm writing here! They are mysterious, confusing creatures. At times, they can be predictable and easy to read well enough to get them to do what you want. Other times, they make you wonder if someone made a Voodoo doll out of them or something. They are emotional. They can be withdrawn and moody. (I guess they can say the same about us.)

I don't know why men cheat. I'm sure there are a thousand reasons or excuses. (There a million and one songs.) But none of them hold water, so, men, save your breath, or drown if you want. I do know that when a woman cheats on a man, she is viewed as far worse than he would be for doing the same thing. We are expected to be submissive and naive yet strong-minded enough to forgive and keep going despite the hurt. Let a woman cheat on her man - he won't know what to do with himself. Yeah, he may try to get back at her with other females, but he will still feel like less of a man no matter how many women he sleeps with after her. The ego is a powerful thing for men. If you stroke it, he will think you're heaven-sent. If you destroy it, he will swear you're the devil's advocate.

Ladies, when you have tears flowing down your cheeks, and you're looking in the mirror, saying to yourself, "I'm beautiful. I have a great body. Everybody loves me. Why did he do that?" - remember that the fault lies with HIM, not with you.

Stress at work. An emotionally distant mother. Boredom. Whatever excuse he offers, it isn't the real reason.

You are beautiful. You are enough. You are loved.

CHAPTER 7

Playing the "Baby card"

Here's something I'll never understand — how something we women have dreamed about all our lives somehow turns out to throw us completely off our games. No, I'm not talking about marriage — don't get me started on that! I'm talking about having children.

What girl didn't play with her dolls, pretending that they were her babies? Whether you went into the Army or studied at Harvard, that "having babies" message is powerful, deep, and meaningful.

There's a reason that women have the "mommy parts."

But still, this isn't the 19th Century anymore. Barefoot and pregnant went out with the horse and buggy, didn't it? Now, women have careers to balance with home life, just like men. (Sometimes even better.)

It's important to plan when you decide to have children. Right?

Right. But that doesn't always stop us from having our careers or our adventurous pursuits sidelined.

That's what happened to Stephanie. She and her live-in boyfriend Keith had been together for five years. They knew that they would have children. They both wanted a family and had talked about it, yet neither one wanted to marry. They just hadn't "gotten around to it yet." In the meantime, they concentrated on building their material lives together and establishing themselves in their careers.

Stephanie was working for a large clothing store chain. Keith was a banker working on investments. They enjoyed the life of a young, successful couple living in the city. They could go out on a weeknight without having to worry about babysitters or anything complex, living a carefree life with no responsibilities except for each other.

As the years passed, their friends were getting married and having babies, then moving to the suburbs. Stephanie and Keith knew that they would do the same. Someday.

One Friday, her boss called her into the office.

"Stephanie, you've really been doing a great job," she said after Stephanie had taken a seat. "The young people's line you championed has been a huge success."

Stephanie smiled. "Thank you."

"No, thank you," her boss said. "You've done all the work. You pushed for that line against some stiff resistance. I think that kind of drive and dedication deserves to be rewarded."

Then, she offered Stephanie a huge promotion to the regional buyer. The position came with a significant raise in salary responsibility and prominence. Stephanie was thrilled. She couldn't wait to tell Barry.

***

On her way home, Stephanie stopped and picked up a bottle of champagne. When she turned the radio on, "I'm Every Woman" by Chaka Khan was playing. She cruised the rest of the way home singing along. That night, when Keith came home, she was waiting for him with a glass of champagne.

***

"What's this?" he asked with a smile as he took the glass she handed him.

"A celebration."

He arched his eyebrows. "A celebration?"

She nodded. Then, as she clinked her glass against his, she described her meeting with her boss. But rather than sharing her excitement, Barry looked down at the floor.

"What's wrong?" she asked. "Don't you think that's great news?"

"Yeah, that's great." The tone is his voice changed noticeably.

"Well then, what's the problem?" she asked, looking at him nervously.

"Well, to tell you the truth, I wanted to talk to you about something tonight, too," he began. I thought it was time we started thinking about starting a family," he said, raising his eyes to hers.

"A baby?" Stephanie said as if the words were vomit coming out of her mouth.

He nodded.

"But I just got promoted!" she yelled.

He didn't say anything. Stephanie felt her million-dollar feeling reduced in a flash to a ten-dollar feeling. All her life, she wanted to have children. She still did. But now? And why did he have to say something right then, right when she wanted to celebrate her promotion? She could hear her sister's voice saying, "I told you he's controlling."

Keith put his arms around her. "Hey, I'm proud of you," he said. "But I'm doing really well. We don't need the extra money. Don't you think it's time we started our family?"

She looked at him, and then she nodded. That night as they laid in bed, Stephanie thought about all of her possibilities with this new promotion. When Keith woke up the next morning, unsure how Stephanie would be feeling, he approached her cautiously.

She was in the kitchen sipping on some tea while singing along to "On My Own" by Whitney Houston.

"Good morning" was said in harmony. Keith didn't know what to make of this. Little did Keith know Stephanie had taken her birth control pill a few minutes before he entered the kitchen.

CHAPTER 8

Do those boobs look real to you?

"Look at that."

I turned in the direction my friend Patti was looking. We were sitting in Starbucks on a busy street. She was looking toward the front of the shop out the window with a view of the main street. I wasn't sure what she meant.

"What?" I asked, my eyes scanning the direction she was looking.

"There, across the street."

I squinted my eyes (I didn't have my glasses on) and tried to focus on what she might have been looking at. "Still, don't see," I confessed.

She let out a breath as if to say, "What's the matter with you anyway?" and then, more helpfully, directed me to the older man walking with a nice-looking and much younger-looking woman.

"How old do you think he is?"

I shrugged. "I don't know, maybe sixty, sixty-five."

"And how old do you think she is?"

I looked again. Damn, I wished I had my glasses. I didn't know why I was straining to look across the street, to begin with. I was more interested in deciding the kind of pie I wanted with my coffee. But the age guessing game was always compelling, so I tried to figure out how old the woman we were looking at might be.

"I don't know, Thirty-five, forty?" I offered my first guess hesitantly.

She let out a breath. "Be real."

I was offended. I was usually pretty good with my age-guessing. I mean, I was at a disadvantage, looking through a window and across the street and not having my glasses, but still, I couldn't be that far off, could I?

"She's twenty-five, if that," Patti said before looking away from the window and stirring her coffee.

"Twenty-five? She looks amazing," I said.

Patti exhaled again. "Anyone can look amazing if they have the money," she said with disdain.

When did women become like cars — getting traded in for the newer model? Okay, I know that's been going on since the beginning of time. But that was mostly just with kings and movie stars. For most everyone else, you stayed with the one you started with. Now, even women in happy marriages are having work done, spicing things up.

Hey, I'm all for spicing things up and keeping it fresh, if you know what I mean. But there is no way other than surgery that these boobs are going to ride on my chest like they did twenty-five years ago! And what's the big deal with a few wrinkles or gray hairs?

I saw an old actress on a talk show the other day, and I swear to God she could barely move her mouth because her skin had been pulled back so tight. She had been shot with so much Botox she couldn't show joy, sadness, or any other emotion if her life depended on it.

But more and more of my friends are considering "going under the knife" for a "touch up." Some of them are widows or divorced and find themselves competing for a handful of available men. Others feel the insult of having salespeople look right through them. Another friend of mine was offended that some construction workers didn't even bother to glance her way.

"I've still got it, don't I?" she asked irately." At least, I still got some of it." Then she shook her head dismissively. "I've forgotten more about loving than those boys I'll ever know!"

I laughed with her but couldn't help feeling the same sense of desperation that lurked behind her boldness. For men, age isn't an obstacle. Gray hair lends an air of dignity. Wrinkles add up to that rough, weathered look. A nice car more than makes up for the inevitable effects of the years on the body.

Not so for women. With the first signs of crow's feet at the corners of our eyes comes worry. The fine lines alongside our lips — smile lines, my ass! — fill us with panic. The sagging boobs, the widened hips, the stretch marks; who could ever find that attractive? Patti turned to her friend and said, where are the men like Barry White singing that bullshit song "I'll Love You Just the Way You Are" Yeah, right! They don't exist.

Attractive is what we want to be! President and CEO of a multibillion-dollar company? I bet she'd trade it all for smooth thighs and a non-dimpled butt.

So, what's a girl to do? How do we keep our husbands and boyfriends from having wandering eyes or, worse, wandering hands? Do we have to go under the knife?

Personally, I am all about a bit of hair coloring, wrinkle-reducing moisturizers, and some well-applied make-up. I am particularly fond of flattering lighting in restaurants. Candlelight works in the bedroom if you can avoid a fire. I draw the line at waxing. That stuff hurts like hell.

I hold out that the part that you have to keep young is your mind and imagination. Nothing makes someone youthful and attractive like laughter. And nothing is more ridiculous than turning our faces and bodies into portraits of what they were when we were younger.

Back to that 'couple' Patti and I saw across the street from Starbucks. Were they happier for all the woman's efforts to look young? Were they together only because she made an effort? Did she really think she was fooling anyone?

Why have we allowed ourselves to turn into the human equivalent of leased cars, where our men think they trade us in (or some version of us) every three years, always opting for the 'newer model?'

There is no newer model. Plus, classics are worth more in value. We are who we are. I can look at people and recognize the beauty of celebrity and youth. But real beauty - that still comes from within.

As we left Starbucks, Patti and I got in her 1967 Corvette while listening to "My Way" by Frank Sinatra.

CHAPTER 9

I love shopping but without him!

One of my favorite things in the world is to go to the mall and go shopping. Sure, the parking lot is like the morning of Black Friday, and people are everywhere, but I get real pleasure from just walking around, looking at things, and window shopping. It's even better when I actually plan on buying something. Yep, I'd say that shopping is one of the best little guilty pleasures in the world - except when my husband tags along with me to the mall.

I'm not saying my husband is not great company. He's a blast. We sing along with the radio when we're in the car together (without the kids, we can listen to our music!) He pretends to be Bradley Cooper, and I'm Lady Gaga, or sometimes, Nick Ashford and Valerie Simpson (depending on our mood.) We workout together; take walks through the park; he is my best friend. But for some reason, shopping is not something we manage to carry out successfully. Usually, it's my fault—silly me. I actually think my husband wants to come to the mall to spend more time with me when he asks where I'm going, and I say shopping.

One particular time I was headed to the mall to start my early Christmas shopping. His eyes lit up.

"That sounds like fun," he said.

Fun? I repeated in my head, almost suspiciously but intrigued that a man would call 'shopping' fun. "You want to come along?"

"Sure!"

I admit I like to get his opinion on how specific clothing looks on me. I never hit him with the famous question that women ask when trying on clothes: "Does this make me look fat?" Throughout our years of honest discussions, his response is always the same. "If you like it, I love it." The trouble is, I might want to go into Intimate Apparel, but he seems to always manage to wander off into the men's department. I wondered if maybe he felt awkwardly out of place because the ladies' underwear section bordered the men's and women's departments. He does tend to get fidgety standing with me while I'm digging through bras and panties. He nearly has a panic attack when other women stop to join me in scanning through the panty pile.

Meanwhile, as I was looking through some blouses and dresses, humming Mariah Carey's "All I Want for Christmas," he had managed to "disappear." When I looked up, he was gone. No surprise there. I'd been married long enough to know that he has a habit of just wandering off.

In the beginning of our marriage, I worried about it, like I would when one of the kids wandered off. When he would return, I'd yell at him, and he would politely listen and simply respond. "I'm a grown-ass man. I am not your child." Over time, I came to understand exactly what he meant. Now when we go shopping, he still disappears, but when he shows up again, he's inevitably got an armful of things -work pants, a couple of shirts, socks, tool gloves, a hat of some description. I no longer worry, and like our trusting cute dog, he comes back.

"What's all that?" I'd asked. "You said you didn't need anything."

He would shrug. "When I was walking around, I saw some things I should get."

"I see." Did I mention that my husband, like almost every man, is something of an impulse shopper? He's like a child (remember that comparison to children and dogs?) who is confronted by a shiny object. They can't turn away or resist their curiosity.

I love my husband, but I suppose it's a good thing the men's department is across the store from the tools and televisions!

CHAPTER 10

When a headache isn't a headache

I'm going to come right out and say it. Sex is good. (Actually, sex is great.) There's a reason why people like it, and most people manage to enjoy sex with their husbands or wives, boyfriends, or girlfriends, etc., without straying outside of the relationship. And yes, too many people — and not just men — spend an awful lot of time devoted to sex on the Internet. (I'll never understand it, sex is personal, physical, intimate, sweaty, and YES, passionate. There are not enough videos that can replace the actual act.) But I think we can agree that sex is a REALLY important part of a relationship.

But sometimes, maybe a lot of the time, you're just not into it.

The simple truth of the matter is that sex is not the same when you're fifty as when you're twenty. First of all, you don't have time for much foreplay. Now, between getting the kids off to school and getting ready for work; cleaning the house; having a drink with friends; cooking dinner; picking up the kids from school and getting them to soccer or basketball practice; doing laundry, and remembering to check in with your mom who hasn't been feeling well, there aren't enough hours in the day for fore-play. There's barely enough time for a kiss on the cheek if you're so inclined. Sometimes, a simple handshake at the door could get your juices flowing if you've been deprived for a while.

When you were seventeen, you spent the whole day thinking about your boyfriend, right? You would doodle his name in your notebook at school, putting your name with his last name, just to see how it would look and sound.

You two would meet at your locker, or his, long enough to steal a kiss between classes, barely making it to the next class without being tardy.

The challenge of finding somewhere private to do anything more than make out increased the sexual tension almost beyond belief. You all know what I'm talking about, ladies. And, of course, there was the dilemma of determining just 'how far' you could go together. Was touching over your shirt and bra okay? What about under your shirt? Oh my God, take off the bra!

Was it any wonder that you were practically melting when he showed up for a date, ready to take you to the movies or a quiet place to park and continue the make-out sessions? Hardly.

And add to that, your hormones were all in a rage.

Well, it's not exactly like that anymore, is it?

You're not doodling names in a notebook all day. You're managing an office, a home, sick patients, or a classroom filled with children. You're worried about making ends meet, or what to fix for dinner, or who's going to pick up little Sean from school and get him to his dentist appointment, or how are you going to get from work to school to pick up Ashley because the school nurse called and she's got a fever.

You're hoping that the unsettled feeling in your stomach is just nerves and not something you ate or the flu or, worst, pregnancy.

Your mind is on a thousand things other than sex.

When you were seventeen, you weren't sure if you were beautiful or if your body was nice enough, but his wanting you so much kind of got you over that hump. Now you know that your body isn't what you want it to be. You don't feel beautiful. You haven't been to the gym in a month. You're mad at yourself for having that slice of Junior's cheesecake. You think your thighs are fat, your butt's too big, your boobs are too small. You're having a slight breakout because you're getting close to your period, or at least you think you are. When did your menstrual cycle get so hard to predict anyway?

You're annoyed that he still doesn't pick up his laundry even after you've asked him/told him to for the last fifteen years. You're grossed out by the skin tag on the back of his neck. And that Captain America tee-shirt...

You wonder what happened to the man you married, the one who got you excited just by being there. And you're really dying to know who's going to win The Voice this week.

By the time you get into bed, you're tired. From the corner of your eye, you see his overweight form strolling toward the bed, and you're already thinking, No way. Not tonight. When did he get that big gut? He's got to lose weight. He missed a spot when he was shaving this morning. I never used to mind that he had a hairy back. Damn, he's got skinny legs. Those boxers are raggedy.

You feel the weight of the bed shift when he gets in. You try not to acknowledge he's there. You set the stage for a good excuse by giving a grimace to make him believe you are in unbearable discomfort. You hope he notices, but you don't want to risk making eye contact.

You can hear the kids are still up even if they are in their rooms, and somehow, the thought of your kids knowing you have sex is even more mortifying than when you were seventeen and saw your parents having sex. What if they walked in when you were having sex?

No decent mother would want to traumatize her children like that. You still shudder in horror when you remember the time your oldest was three, and he happened to wander into the bedroom in the middle of the night.

"No, mommy and daddy aren't fighting, honey. We're just playing around. What's the matter anyway? Why are you up? No, you can't come into the bed, not right now. Go back to your room. I'll be right there to tuck you in."

Now, there are more reasons not to have sex than to have sex. You're thinking about what you have to do tomorrow, what you didn't get done today, what the kids have to do tomorrow, what you're going to make for dinner tomorrow, or even on Saturday. You feel panicky. You sure don't feel sexy. And then you feel his body shift. You know that shift all too well. It's not just rolling over in bed. This is a signal. He wants some.

"Hey."

"Hey yourself."

"How're you?"

"Tired, and I have a headache," you say. You're careful to say it, so he doesn't automatically think it's a code.

You want him to know that you really are tired,

"You take something?"

"Yeah, a little while ago."

"Did it help?"

"Not yet."

"Can I do anything?"

"No, I don't think so. Thanks." It was sweet of him to ask.

***

Meanwhile, you want to sing at the top of your vocals Regina's Bell, "Make It Like It Was."

***

He rests his hand on your thigh and gives it a gentle squeeze. You know he's just showing affection, but you hate when he squeezes that part of your thigh, where all the loose fat is. It just makes you think about how you haven't been to the gym.

"Hey," he says again, massaging your thigh.

"I don't think so," you say, trying to sound caring. "My head is really killing me. It hurts even to move my head."

He doesn't stop. Not yet. No matter how much is going on, it takes a lot to get your man to say no to sex. He's not going to give up without a fight, and just realizing that somehow gets your mind focused on all the negatives about him. That skin tag. The hair in his ears. The patch of eczema on his back.

You can't remember when you last thought he was handsome or when he made you feel like the guy on the television does. You feel a momentary revulsion as you realize that, at that moment, you cannot stand to look at him.

"I married this?" you think to yourself. "My God, what was I thinking?"

You close your eyes tight. "Headache," you say again, a bit more insistently.

He withdraws his hand. His weight shifts a bit more to his side of the bed. He finally gets the message, and as you fall asleep, you're singing in your head the lyrics, "make it like it was/ the way it used to be/ when I hungry for your love, constantly." Feeling guilty, you make a mental note to suggest a "date night" this weekend. Maybe send the kids to grandma's house. You would have to think about it and not make any sudden decision in case you change your mind.

But for now, that headache is definitely a problem.

CHAPTER 11

I'm Lucky!

Just when you think, if your man does that thing he does that drives you absolutely crazy one more time, you're going to hit him over the head with a frying pan, something happens that makes you realize that you're the luckiest gal in the world to have him.

At least that was how CeCe felt not too long ago.

For a stretch, it seemed like everything Mario did just irked the hell out of her. The funny noise he made in the back of his throat when his allergies were bothering him. The smell of his aftershave, his mismatched socks, or how he wore brown shoes with black pants.

It drove CeCe crazy when a pretty girl would walk by, and he would look at her and say, "She's pretty." Well, duh! It's evident to everyone that she's pretty.

Does he really have to comment or state the obvious? It's not like he does it to make CeCe jealous or that he's interested in the girl. He is just stating the obvious, like "it's a beautiful day" on a beautiful day. But it bothered her just the same. She was not fond of him taking on the role of "Captain Obvious."

She was also annoyed with his slurping when he ate soup and his snoring. Not to mention the way he drove. She couldn't stand how he drove. He'd drive too fast and then have to hit the brakes all fast. Once, she spilled coffee on herself because he stopped so suddenly after tailgating the car in front of them. When he came to an intersection, and the light was changing, he'd race through instead of coming to a stop.

"Why do you drive like that?" she'd ask him, clearly frustrated.

"You don't want me to drive like a little old lady, do you?" he'd laugh.

***

She'd fume. Was he suggesting that she was a little old lady? And why did he have to play the sports station on the radio whenever they were in the car? Couldn't he put on something she liked?

And he spent way too much time with his tools in the garage just not to fix or build a damn thing.

CeCe could find a million things that drove her crazy about Mario. However, one nasty winter day, she was getting out of her car, slipped on some ice, and broke her ankle. The look on Mario's face when he showed up at the emergency room melted her heart.

"It's only my ankle," she said, laughing.

"What happened? You didn't hurt anything else?"

She shook her head. It took her breath away when she realized just how much he cared about her, how much he loved her. Sure, he didn't say it so much anymore; that happens after many years of marriage. But she could see it in his face and how his voice caught when he asked the doctor if she was all right.

Until she had healed enough to get a walking cast and could move around on her own, he took care of everything. He helped her get into the shower, making sure her cast was wrapped in plastic. He cooked dinner. He shopped. He went to the video store and made sure she had plenty of old movies to watch during the day.

In short, he treated her like a queen.

He still made that funny noise in his throat. He still slurped his soup. He still snored. He still wore mismatched socks. And in the evening, when they watched television together, he pointed out when a pretty actress came on the screen.

You know what? Suddenly, that stuff didn't bother CeCe at all. She just smiled and turned to him. "Could you get me a cup of tea, please?"

"Sure thing," he said, like he couldn't do enough for her fast enough, "You want anything else with that?"

He put in grab bars in the bathroom and tightened the rails on the stairs so that she could feel more comfortable. But he didn't make her feel like he was doing it because she wasn't 't steady on her feet anymore. No, he said he wasn't getting any younger. That day CeCe realized how lucky she indeed was as they sat and ate dinner. She thought about Anita Baker's "Just Because" and dedicated that song to him.

That winter, he shoveled the steps and the sidewalk, so they were as clean as a whistle.

***

Billie had a similar experience. She and Justin had been married twenty-six years. Like most people, after twenty-six years, you start to take an awful lot for granted. The things that make you happy get dulled a bit, and the things that annoy you seem exaggerated. You start to forget just how much you depend on that other person.

Billie's sister, Karen, lost her husband a few months ago. It was a terrible time for the family. Karen is a few years younger than Billie. Her husband suffered a heart attack at work. After the initial, intense grief passed,

Karen's greatest regret was that she hadn't noticed when he'd left for work that morning.

"I didn't say goodbye. I didn't say I loved him. For all I knew, he was just going out to get the paper. I don't even remember for sure the last time I saw him," Karen added, with tears in her eyes. "Was it when he was putting on his socks? Pouring coffee? Coming in after taking out the garbage?"

"Don't be so hard on yourself," Billie advised. Karen ignored her. "But you know the worst thing? Just how big the bed feels now that I'm the only one in it." Her voice was so filled with sadness and loneliness when she said that. Billie hugged her tightly.

That night, when Billie got into bed, she moved closer to her husband, so glad and grateful to feel his bulk and warmth there with her.

There's no question that men are the most annoying, frustrating, pesky creatures in the world sometimes, but they can be rocks when you need them to be. And sometimes, when you catch your man out of the corner of your eye, and the sunlight hits him just right, you find yourself smiling. "Yeah," you mentally start singing, "You Bring Me Joy," and blurt out, "he is kinda cute."

CHAPTER 12

I didn't know I wanted him

Growing up in Queens was interesting for Yvette. Like most girls from the area, she fell hard for the bad boys in the neighborhood. But unlike most girls, she was determined to get her education and move away. Perhaps it was her strict upbringing, tenacity, or simply wanting more and being better.

Yvette went away to school, and while on summer break, she returned home, back to the neighborhood she longed to leave behind. However, this summer would be the beginning of a life she thought she did not want or a man she didn't even like.

He was the total opposite of what she was accustomed to. He took some getting used to, like a new pair of heels that didn't quite fit right but had to be broken in. At first sight, she was not attracted to him, but something intrigued her about him. Gerald had always found Yvette interesting and sexy, and he was determined to win her over.

As Yvette recalled, his name should have been Persistent than Gerald. He finally convinced her to go on a date, and they went to see "Boyz 'N' The Hood." To her surprise, he made her laugh, and their conversations were effortless. She found herself looking forward to seeing him again. She returned to college but found herself thinking about him more than she cared to admit. She looked forward to Thanksgiving break, just to see him, although she never admitted it.

While hanging with some of her friends from high school, she overheard Kelly, one of the local girls, talking about how Phyllis was trying to work her "magic" on Gerald. This bothered Yvette a lot, even though she knew that Phyllis was not exactly competition. What bothered her the most was that she did not know how Gerald truly felt about her. She knew that he was into her, but she was unsure if those feelings were strong enough to resist females like Phyllis.

The next day when Gerald came by, they watched a movie together. He kissed her on the cheek and left. She quickly ran to the window to watch him leave. She was falling for him. As she stared out, she immediately noticed Phyllis approaching him. (Whenever Yvette tells the story, she chuckles.) She ran down those stairs so quickly and made her presence known. She was claiming

Gerald as her man, announcing that he was off-limits to the prowlers.

Every anniversary, she plays Toni Braxton's "I Love Me Some Him." They are happily married with three beautiful children, and yes, he constantly reminds her of how much she didn't want him.

WOMEN & CHILDREN

Every moment leading up to motherhood is like walking across a minefield. From the planning (if you planned) to the conception (whether it was natural or artificial,) and finally learning that you are pregnant - is a process that leaves you emotionally and physically invested like no other experience. It is the calm before the storm. And when you hear your baby cry for the first time, and they lay him or her (or them!) in your arms, you realize it was worth all the chaos.

Everything about being a mother involves you in a chain of existence going back to the women who came before you, then from you to your children. Because of this inevitable connection, you strive to do everything right, which usually means you swear to do things differently than your mother did them. The moment you realize that you've said or done something to your children that your mother said or did to you growing up, it makes you cringe and question how it happened. It's funny how things turn out, especially when you try so hard to avoid them.

We want to be better parents for our kids, but we want to be better parents for our own parents, too.

Our children are our gift to the generations that came before us - a gift that keeps on giving and taking.

And we're the ones that have to be there to clean up the mess!

CHAPTER 13

The beginning

Pregnancy is like a box of chocolates. You never know what you're going to get. For some, the experience is pleasant. For others, it is tolerable. However, for the rest, it makes them want to get their tubes tied immediately after the cord is cut.

The beginning is exciting! You are anxious and engaged in how much your body is changing or not changing. You stand in the mirror, rubbing your belly, slightly pushing it out, trying to visualize how you will look when the bump really starts to show. But for now, the only physical difference you notice is your breasts. And they are getting huge! You think about the years you wanted your boobs to be bigger, but you don't exactly feel sexy now that they are. Why not? Because the damn things hurt! They are tender, sore, and your bras fit like you're a teenager who hasn't gotten rid of her training bras. But despite that, you feel feminine, miraculous, and powerful. There's a human growing inside you!

It is such a confusing time in your life. You listen to other women and hear about their experiences with their pregnancies. One woman swears she climaxed during childbirth. You did not think that was possible. Actually, you find it crazy as hell. I mean, what woman in her right mind is turned on in a room of strangers, taking turns feeling in her vagina checking for crowning. But to each their own. Then, of course, you can't forget about your aunt, who said she pushed out something brown and wet from the front and the back. TMI.

As the months go by, you look forward to discovering what your body is doing or what your baby could be doing. Your friend at work who has enough kids for a family basketball team gives you a book called,

What to Expect When You're Expecting. It becomes your bible. You are mesmerized by the pictures and intrigued by the information. You compare your body to the figure in the book, imagining how you will look in your final trimester. However, you have no idea if you will gain weight because you can barely keep anything down – except Pistachio ice cream with salsa. Sometimes, you and the baby agree on chicken burritos, too.

As your weight starts to pick up drastically, you decide that maybe you should at least try to be healthy and spare yourself any unnecessary 'baby fat' that will take you years to get rid of. You have a friend who is also pregnant and attends yoga about four days a week. She is into it a little too much. You wonder what in the world she is sometimes thinking.

"Girl, I'm not about to put my foot way back there," you say, staring at her like she's the main event in a freak show.

She rolls her eyes. "I don't see why not. You did it before. That's why you looking how you looking now with that belly, Ms. Thang," she teases.

So, you try yoga, even Lamaze classes. Your husband is so supportive. He rubs your swollen feet and ankles and even ties your shoes. You confide in him that you are scared about giving birth.

"What if I can't push? What if I need a c-section?" you worry out loud.

He assures you, "Woman, you are not the first female to do this. Your body is structured to have kids. You will be fine," he kisses your forehead. "It's going to hurt so bad. What if my stuff doesn't shrink back?"

He is silent, then says, "Oh, yeah. You better start those Kegel exercises like right now!" he laughs. "I got a monster, but I can't compete with no six-pound, seven-pound baby.

Once in a while, you catch him looking at you. You wonder if he is staring because you have gotten so big.

You don't feel attractive. Your nose is getting huge, and you look big as a house in the mirror. The times he wants to be intimate, you think he is only doing it because he has needs. You don't think he sincerely finds you sexy anymore. Sure, he's enjoying the double size of your breasts, but having sex when you're pregnant is weird. You almost feel guilty. What if you hurt the baby? What if the baby knows what's going on? You anticipate when it's over so that you can be a 'good mother' again.

No matter how common it is, being pregnant brings attention from strangers or people who would probably never speak to you. They ask you how far along you are, your due date; are you having a boy or a girl. Sometimes, they request to touch your stomach. You don't mind, and you really feel like a superstar when your baby kicks and they feel it.

"Oh, my goodness! That was so cool. Does it hurt?"

You tell them it only hurts when you are lying down on your side, and the baby kicks you in your rib cage. Your husband has a trick for that, though. He rubs ice where the baby kicks to make it move away. Throughout the pregnancy, he has been your rock until the day you're in active labor, and those contractions are kicking your ass, and you wish you had some rocks to throw at him.

"I hate you! I hate you! Don't you ever think that you're ever going to touch me again because you're not!"

He ignores you like he was told to in the birthing class you took. He even feeds you ice chips and tells you to breathe in through your nose and out through your mouth. He calmly asks you to relax your toes.

You tell him to shut up, followed by some choice words.

"Get out of here, get away from me. I hate you!" You continue to protest.

And you mean it with every fiber of your being. Just like you mean it when you cry to the heavens above to get the demon child out of your body when the doctor says, "Push!" And then, a few minutes later, you hold your brand-new baby in your arms. "Speechless" by Alicia Keys fills its melody in your head. You smile at your husband and your baby, and you believe that you are the most blessed person in all of creation.

CHAPTER 14

Give me a break, Mom!

B abies are the gifts we give our parents. To become a mother is to bond with our own mothers in ways we could never have imagined, to join a sisterhood that transcends time or place. It is instinctual. It is deep. It is real. It also involves buying a lot of cute baby clothes.

Gwen had missed her period for the last two months. That wasn't all that unusual for her. She was irregular in the best of times - not that that didn't cause some worrying days when she was younger and dating! But over the years, she had gotten used to her pattern. She and Dave had wanted to get pregnant for a year or so, not in a determined way but in a "wouldn't it be nice to have kids" sort of way. So, every time they had sex, it was kind of in the back of her mind.

Gwen and I would discuss her desire or lack of desire to have children based on other people's motivation.

"My mom has been driving me crazy ever since she found out how 'serious' we were, how she was looking forward to being a grandmother. She used to do this thing where she'd say how cute our children would be, with my hair and Dave's eyes. That kind of thing. It is so annoying."

"I know, but your mom is just excited for you," I had said, careful not to appear to take sides.

"I bet she is," Gwen had laughed. "But she was quick to add that we shouldn't rush anything until we are married. It didn't seem to bother her that we were living together, but when it came to children and becoming a grandmother, she wanted to get all traditional."

Even when Gwen called to tell her that Dave had proposed, the idea of having children, making her a grandmother was right there.

"She said how happy she was for us," Gwen had explained. "Then she added that now we could have children as if I needed her permission! Girl, bye."

I shook my head at her and chuckled a little. Gwen was very candid when it came to talking about her mother, or about anyone for that matter. If something bothered her, she would vent until she got it all out. I felt like I was her therapist.

"Even in all the excitement of the wedding, there were still comments. My mom was happy that I was getting married. She loved Dave and welcomed him into her arms like a son, but she was focused on 'the prize.' She wanted to be a grandmother.

This made me wonder if my mother wanted another chance at 'parenting' since she was so busy with school or focusing on her career when my brother and I were little." Gwen had been clearly frustrated with her mother's intentions, but she had to understand the method behind the madness. However, her mom was not doing much to help her case.

They'd no sooner gotten back from the honeymoon before her mother started in with the "well?" conversation starter.

"Well, what?" Gwen had teased her, knowing exactly what "well" meant and what it was for. Gwen tended to mess with her mother from time to time. Again, her mother repeated, "Well?" to which Gwen replied, "Mom, I don't think you can handle the details. It would be too much for you to bear."

Gwen's mom had rolled her eyes, "Child, please. How do you think you got here? If walls and mirrors could talk…" she laughed. "But Gwen, stop playing with me. You know what I'm talking about."

The truth was the idea that Gwen should one day make her mother a grandmother hardly began when she was seriously dating Dave. The hints, cues, and desires had been implanted in her mind and emotions since she was a little girl. It was no wonder that she had already begun thinking of a baby as much for her mother as for her and Dave.

Gwen had told me: "We were both working hard to establish ourselves. We had been living together for years, but for some reason, being married, that certificate, made it seem all new. We were in that blissful first year of marriage. Still, I knew I wasn't getting any younger."

Sometimes, when in Walgreens, Gwen would wander around and end up in the aisle with the pregnancy testing kits. Although she knew she had plenty of kits at home, she seemed to always purchase another kit. She thought to herself, "by the time I do conceive, I'll be broke from the number of pregnancy kits I bought." Still, each time she was nervous and excited.

"What am I thinking of?" she corrected herself. "I've always been irregular with my period."

By the time she reached for one of the kits, she didn't know what she wanted more - a positive result or a negative one. "Going to the bathroom had never been a more nerve-wracking experience," she had confided in me.

"My hands were shaking. I dropped the dipstick thingy on the floor. Then I worried that that might affect the results."

She explained this story to me with laughter. At the time, she was frantic, rushing across the bathroom with her pants and panties below her knees, pinching the thin stick between her fingers, and prying it up off the tile floor. Then she sat down on the toilet, took a deep breath, and started.

A few seconds later. "Oh, my God!"

She was pregnant. She finished, jumped up, pulled up her pants, and, having been raised properly, washed her hands. She yelled for her mom, realizing, of course, that she was home alone. Dave wasn't home at the time. She had purposefully waited until after he'd work to do the pregnancy test. She hadn't told him that she thought she was pregnant. They had been through the excitement and disappointment too many times. She hadn't even got out of the bathroom before she took out her cell phone. Pausing to catch her breath and calm her excitement, she dialed her mother's phone number.

"Hi, Mom. Sitting down?" her heart feeling like it would beat out of her chest.

She had given some thought to how she wanted to tell her mother that she was pregnant.

She thought, maybe something clever like, "What do you want your grandchild to call you?" or "Are you sure you're old enough to be a grandmother?" She thought about asking what she wanted her vanity plates to read. Or if she was ready to wear frumpy, "old lady" shoes.

As soon as her mother picked up the phone, the tears started pouring down. Gwen thought back to all the times her mom played "In My Daughter's Eyes." She was so overwhelmed with emotions that she could not speak. Of course, this alarmed her mother.

"Gwen? Hello? Are you all right?"

"Yes, yes. I'm good," Gwen managed to stammer out between tears. "I'm pregnant, Mom! I'm pregnant!"

Her mother didn't say anything. She was crying, too.

Be careful what you wish for.

CHAPTER 15

Which brings me back to pregnancy

Everyone has a pregnancy story- ankles swelling to the size of tree trunks, not being able to reach the steering wheel because your belly forces you to push the seat back too far, having to pee every two minutes. (Did I say "every two minutes?" More like every thirty seconds!) You will be convinced your soon-to-be baby is the Devil's spawn because she/he won't stop using your insides for a punching bag. You wonder what in the hell is inside of you. You fear you're going to turn out like Sigourney Weaver when she gives birth to an alien monster.

But none of that comes close to the real insult of pregnancy. Want to know the real insult? The look. The look? "You know the look," my friend Ashley told me when I was about seven months along. "Don't tell me you don't know the look."

I lowered my eyes because I couldn't fix them in her direction.

Come on, ladies. Let's not play games; we're too deep into this. You know the look, too- the one in your husband's eyes. That man who once upon a time, could not keep his hands off you, who whispered the most delightful and inappropriate things in your ear, no longer has any problem keeping his hands to himself. The man who knew which song turned you from the "good girl" image into something very naughty now only plays Ed Sheeran's "Thinking Out Loud" and looks at you like a cute little puppy.

Ashley basically told me that I was no longer the object of my husband's desire. She elaborated, "He no longer lusts for you but "appreciates" you as the woman who will soon be the mother of his child. He loves you. Absolutely. Maybe more than ever. But the love has changed. There is less lust and hunger and more warmth and caring."

Desire and lust are the reason you're in this situation. You become paranoid enough to think that's a bad thing, which you translate into the fact that he's probably cheating on you because you've gained so much weight and are hideously unattractive.

I had tried to convince myself that the reason I was receiving "the look" was because of my moodiness. You know how we get when our hormones are all over the place, especially with pregnancy. Even the horniest man would probably pass on some ass to avoid dealing with your insecure, nasty, indecisive, moody, emotional butt.

Interestingly, food and mood not only rhyme but also play a dynamic coed role in pregnancy. You go through the weird food cravings and throw a fit if you can't get it. So, your supportive partner goes out in the middle of the night on the hunt for something like eggnog in May when you know damn well that's a seasonal drink. Yet, he caters and accommodates you. But, it's not really you making all this fuss, right? It's the baby's fault. The same baby, sixteen years later, will give you the exact attitude and backtalk you gave your parents. Surprise! But none of this justifies you to be over the top with him for every single thing.

But do you really want to be intimate, anyway? You've got heartburn like you've eaten Hot and Spicy noodles all day. To top it off, you haven't had a bowel movement in so long you can't tell if it's the baby kicking or gas. When you call your mother, she warns you that constipation will only get worse. Her advice? Prunes. Prunes, you think to yourself. Am I eighty years old?

As you lay in bed, you're still wondering why he hasn't touched you in months, and for one split second, you conceive to the reality of your behavior and admit, "I wouldn't want to touch me either." Now, Nicole got pregnant after getting remarried. A new husband. A new family.

Whatever emotional trauma she had gone through with her divorce, she could finally put behind her.

One would think.

In addition to her new husband and baby to come, Nicole was dealing with her teenage daughter from her first marriage. The relationship between mothers and their adolescent daughters becomes complex during these years (we discuss this further in the teenage years) and add to it pregnancy. The emotions from both sides of the aisle heighten to a level which one would never imagine.

Wouldn't it be great if mothers always sought healthy ways to do this?

As is often the case with teenage girls, body image was a constant issue. Nicole's daughter was worried that her butt was too big and that she was 'too fat.' She had dedicated herself to a strict diet and exercise program. Determined to 'bond' with her daughter, she chose her pregnancy to diet with her daughter! Every morning she worked-out with her daughter to Beyonce's song "Run the World." After the song was over and Nicole sat down to catch her breath, her daughter would say, "I don't think so, Ma." They would both break out in a burst of hysterical laughter. What was she thinking? Now was not the time to see how little she could gain.

Dieting is a foundational issue for women. Let's face it, the women who don't think they could lose a few pounds are few and far between. I don't have a single friend who would say that her rear isn't too big if asked and answered honestly. Most of us spend a lifetime struggling to come to terms with and hopefully falling in love with our bodies and selves. Too many women are never successful. But please, please, please, whatever your body image issues, do not allow them to play out during pregnancy! You are going to get big during your pregnancy.

Let a good, sensible doctor guide you!

You will get bigger during your pregnancy. It is inevitable, and you should get bigger. You have a little butterball baby growing in that belly of yours. Your internal organs will be moved all-around. You will have a baby's head pressing against your bladder all the time. Your hips will widen. Your skin will stretch. Your formerly 'innie' belly button will pop out and become an 'outie.' Think bigger and happier, not fat!

As your body changes, don't make yourself crazy, sticking to your old routines. You're changing. Accept it. Embrace it. Love it. Change your routines to match your new reality.

THE SECOND TRIMESTER[1]

The second trimester is a wonderful time to think about a baby shower. You still feel good. You've got some balance from your initial joy. You're over the mood swings (most days.) You're not the size of a house yet. You've got your energy back. It's an excellent time to enjoy a party. Of course, you won't. Not yet. You're still superstitious. Okay, I get it. We've all been there. Don't paint the baby's room yet. Don't put up the crib. Don't have anything for the baby in the house. Don't give it a name. Don't let me know its sex.

We protect ourselves from the fear that something might go wrong in a thousand different ways. And if you think I'm going to tell you that you're being ridiculous, you're wrong. I'm all good with all the peculiar things we do to keep our heads screwed on relatively straight, especially when we're pregnant. You want to wrap red yarn around the crib. Go ahead. You want to wait until the baby is a week old to give it a name. No problem. You don't want to know your baby's gender. That's your business. Or if you want to know but prefer not to tell anyone – hey, that's your prerogative, as Bobby Brown would tell you. Embrace whatever makes you most comfortable.

Having a baby brings about enough changes in your body and your life. Create a comfort zone and stay in it as much as you can. Because I'll tell you what, being pregnant is an amazing, life-altering experience, but it rarely resembles what you think it will.

THE THIRD TRIMESTER

The third trimester, or the finishing line, as I liked to call it, is where things can really get tough. Everything and everybody bothers you. You feel like you're back in the first trimester, only worse, You're carrying more weight, so your back is sorer. Your legs are tender. Your bladder is getting pressed on more. Your stomach feels the size of a thimble, so no matter what you, it eat gives you heartburn.

Your baby's got his/her head shoved right up under your ribs, making it hard to take a deep breath, so naturally, you feel short of breath. If you're like my girl Keisha, you suffered from hemorrhoids during your pregnancy and announced that it was worse than heartburn, 'the look,' weight gain, and morning sickness... She absolutely hated it.

You feel fat. And since I'm one to keep it real, you probably look fat, too. Therefore, everyone else looks so thin. Yet, you seem to forget or ignore that you are pregnant and gaining weight is natural. So, if you feel fat, it's for a reason – an extremely good one, at that. Yes, you see all of these skinny girls walking around in their cute little clothes, showing off their bodies. You miss being cute. You miss dressing sexy. But you can't do any of that until you get this baby the hell out of you.

Remember, babies are the gifts we give our parents. To be a mother is to bond with our own mothers in ways we could never have imagined by joining a sisterhood that transcends time or place. It is visceral. It is deep. It is real.

I know I said that before. I want to say it again because it's important. It's the reason that we go through these long months of joy, annoyance, discomfort, fear, exhilaration, pride, and unbelievable anticipation. It is the reason we never miss our check-ups, and we endure ultrasounds (listening for the reassuring thump, thump, thump of our baby's heartbeat). It is the reason we flop ourselves down on the examination table, slip our feet into the stirrups, and let it all hang out for every doctor, nurse, and person who can help us end up with a healthy, happy baby.

CHAPTER 16

The miracle of birth...

O r, how did I ever fit a bowling ball through there!

Rachel, fifty-two months pregnant (at least, that's how she felt,) was ready. She was more than ready. She was "stick-a-fork-in-it" ready. She'd been waddling about for so long that she could hardly remember a time when she could walk standing straight up or a time when she could look down and actually see her feet. She'd been through it all, the entire roller coaster ride of pregnancy — the thrill when she first found out, the morning sickness, and finally the unnecessarily enormous boobs. Her belly button popped out, and her hips widened. She always wanted more of an hour-glass figure, but her pregnant proportion made her look like a sippy-cup instead. Her bladder shrunk. She couldn't eat a bite without burping.

She'd had ultrasounds and more doctor visits than she'd had in her previous twenty-seven years. She had an amnio because she wasn't sure that the virus she'd had during her early pregnancy didn't affect the baby.

As she laid down waiting for her ultrasound, singing Reba McEntire's song "You're Gonna Be," she felt her heart stop when the technician couldn't find the baby's heartbeat.

"Ooops," the technician smiled guiltily, realizing that she accidentally unplugged the probe.

It took her twenty minutes to calm down from that visit! Trevor would pay for this!

She'd gone through the excitement of feeling the baby's first kicks and was way over him or her, sticking whatever body part they wanted in her ribs, which made it painful to breathe.

One night while sleeping in the den - if you can call it sleeping – Rachel could not find a comfortable position to save her life. Trevor, of course, was exhausted. He had been working late to ensure he had time off for when the baby came. Not to mention, he had painted, cleaned, and prepared everything for the baby's arrival. Rachel reasoned that he might also be tired from dealing with her mood swings. It could be draining, after all. So, when Trevor had fallen asleep around 9 o'clock, Rachel could not complain. The man was whipped, and he deserved the rest.

Lying there on the easy-chair, Rachel felt something she had never felt before. It was like an electric jolt, followed by cramping. It was strange and indescribable but also new and frightening.

Could this be, she thought. She didn't want to think about it. Not yet. She was scared to move. So, just waited - two minutes, five. Then it happened again. It lasted only a few seconds. But it happened.

"Oh, my God! Oh, my God!"

She pushed herself up from the chair and waddled toward the bedroom. "Trevor, Trevor!" He jumped up from a sound sleep like he'd been hit with a cattle prod. "Huh? What's wrong?" he asked, looking around as if someone had intruded in their home.

"I think it's time."

Rachel laughed at Trevor, running around in the half-dark, looking for his glasses and trying to put his pants on over his pajama bottoms. At the same time, he was hopping on one foot toward the bag that they had packed, ready by the front door.

"Are you all right?" he asked, breathless and anxious. "What's happening?"

She was still laughing as she was about to answer when another contraction hit. This one was more intense than the previous contractions.

"What just happened?" he asked, the color draining from his face.

"I think I just had a contraction," she said.

"Come on! Let's go!" he screamed as if the baby might arrive any second.

That made her laugh again. "It's all right," she said. "We've got a ways to go." At least, she hoped so. They both took a couple of deep breaths and then got organized. About half an hour and a couple of good contractions later, they were in the car headed towards the hospital. The car ride seemed so surreal for Rachel. It was like it was happening, but not to her-like watching a movie. She made a mental note to live in the moment so she could always remember this night. Yet, there was so much going through her mind. What if I can't push hard enough? What if I push too hard out the wrong hole? Or what if I pass out altogether?

Her mind brought her back to the present, and she noticed Trevor, who didn't know whether he wanted to drive like a lunatic or like he was driving Miss Daisy. He glanced at her every two seconds, holding her hand so Rachel could squeeze it during contractions.

Rachel reflected on the other times they'd driven to the hospital. Trevor being Trevor, they had driven to the hospital tons of times, exploring different routes at different times during the day. They had also gone to the hospital many times for Lamaze class and the maternity ward tour.

"This is really about to happen!"

Rachel exclaimed."Breathe," Trevor said, still sharing his focus between Rachel and the road every two seconds.

"Like this, remember?" he showed her, breathing in through his nose then out through pursed lips as they had learned in class.

When they got to the hospital, he stopped at the main entrance and walked Rachel in. When they announced to the information officer what was happening, she smiled warmly and excitedly and retrieved a wheelchair for Rachel. Then she called up to the maternity ward.

"A nurse will be right down," she said to Rachel. Then she looked at Trevor. "You go park your car and then meet your wife upstairs."

Trevor looked at Rachel with uncertainty about leaving her alone. She gave him a reassuring nod, and he was out the door. Before Trevor even got in the car, the elevator door opened, and a smiling nurse's aid came out to meet Rachel and wheel her upstairs.

"How are you doing?" she asked in a bubbly voice. Rachel's contractions were beginning to get shorter, and she wasn't the nicest patient. She turned to the nurse and sarcastically replied, "How do you think I'm doing? I'm about to have a baby. I'm in pain!"

Just then, another contraction hit, stronger and longer-lasting. The nurse's aide nodded, "Let's get upstairs and see what's going on." This time Rachel kept her comments to herself, but she mocked the nurse aid in her mind. "See what's going on? Are you an idiot? I'm having a baby." By the time Trevor got upstairs and found where his wife was, she was already in an examination room, draped in a flimsy hospital gown and her feet in the all-too-familiar stirrups. Her contractions were coming a bit more regularly and lasting a little longer when they arrived. However, she had hardly dilated, and her water had yet to break.

The doctor spoke with both of them. "I think it will be a while longer," he said with a smile. "But it's a borderline call whether to send you back home to walk around or keep you here."

"Here!" both Rachel and Trevor said at once, neither interested in being in each other's company but for different reasons.

The doctor laughed. "Okay. But I want you walking around. Try to move this early labor along."

Rachel and Trevor felt like they were putting in miles along the hospital corridor. Rachel believed she knew every tile on the floor, every piece of artwork on the walls, every crash cart, every common area in the entire hospital. As expected, the contractions continued and became stronger. But they were still manageable. Nothing she couldn't function through.

The doctor was pleased with the progress a couple of hours later when he reassessed.

She was dilating. "Everything looks good," he said. "Moving in the right direction."

It had been too late to call her mother when they left for the hospital, and so they walked their way through the night until the early morning, the contractions growing in length and intensity.

At seven in the morning, Rachel called her mom to tell her she was at the hospital and let her know what was happening. Rachel was excited, but she was also exhausted. She'd only caught a few naps through the night. She had not gotten more than a couple of hours of light sleep between the walking and the contractions.

She and Trevor were walking in the hallway when she felt something funny. Although she had never in her life actually peed her pants, she knew that that was exactly how it felt. Her legs were wet. Her eyes widened, and she looked down at the floor. There was a puddle at her feet!

"Oh my God!"

Her water had broken. It's funny what being the husband of a woman about to give birth does to perfectly normal, capable men. They might be mechanics, lawyers, teachers, or corporate heads. In their daily lives, they make rational decisions all the time. They are in charge. In command. After all, isn't that what they mean when they say they're acting 'like men.' Well, that changes pretty dramatically when their wives are about to give birth. Basically, it turns them into total fools!

Trevor was a man capable of managing an entire division at work, of dealing with just about any emergency that came up — at work or outside of work. One time, he saw an accident near a park, a bicyclist hit by a car, and he stayed with the person until the ambulance arrived, keeping them safe. The entire time, he was a strong, calming presence.

But as soon as he looked down and saw that Rachel's water had broken, a high-pitched scream exploded from his throat, and he sang like an Opera singer "Nurse!"

Of course, the nurse came running over and immediately helped Rachel back to her room while instructing building services to clean the hallway.

Once in the stirrups again, it was clear that Rachel had continued to progress. It was time for the 'fun' to begin. When lying there in such a vulnerable state, a woman in labor will evaluate many things. So, when Trevor – her sweet and kind husband – leaned over all lovey-dovey, talking that "Baby, breathe" crap, she wanted to choke him. His handsome face was contorted into an evil mask. The man who had touched her in the most intimate ways, whose touch she loved, had become the Devil in her eyes.

"'Get away from me!' she screamed at him, not able to withstand his kindness, concern, or his love. "You did this to me!"

To Rachel, it felt like her insides were being pulled inside out.

"You're doing great," the doctor said.

"Shut up!" she shouted.

"Really great," he continued in a nice, even voice. "You're doing just fine."

He wasn't thrown by her hysterics. He'd been through this before. But poor Trevor was shocked at the change that had come over his wife. His gentle, loving Rachel sounded like she was possessed! As for Rachel herself, she was caught up in an endless loop of prayer:

'Dear Lord, let me have this baby, and I will never, ever, ever do this again. I will sleep in a separate room from Trevor. I will never let him touch me again.'

"I promise!" she said aloud before realizing it.

The contractions just kept coming. Over and over. More and more intense. With less time in between for her to relax.

Trevor repeated his go-to mantra, "Breath." And she replied her usual, "Shut up!"

"Now! Push!" the doctor instructed.

Exhausted, at her wit's end and without much strength to argue, she pushed. Rachel could not think of how to describe the following moments. Pain. Release. Relief. Then, a second later, they heard a baby crying. Euphoria!

Trevor was crying and kissing Rachel. She was crying and laughing. They then brought her baby girl to her and laid her on top of Rachel's chest. The baby instantly gravitated toward a breast and began to suck.

Becoming a mother was an experience that took the words out of Rachel's mouth. She felt as though the heavens opened up, and all the angels sang joyful songs in dedication to her baby girl. She was a mommy! Her family felt so complete with Trevor telling her how much he loved her and their new baby.

"Baby, you did amazing," Trevor said admirably. "Next time around, you'll be spitting 'em out like sunflower seeds," he joked.

Rachel rolled her eyes, "Whatever, Trevor," but the idea of having more children crossed her mind briefly. Nah, she thought to herself.

CHAPTER 17

Something's wrong-

D o you remember when you were in junior high school, and your feelings were always magnified? If a friend passed you in the hallway without stopping to talk, it was the end of the world because they suddenly 'hated' you. If your mom said "No" to you about polishing your nails or wearing a skirt above your knees, you had an attitude for three days. You would complain about how unfair she was and how other girls were wearing the same skirt. Your mom would throw at you that infamous comeback line that drove you crazy. "I don't care what other girls do." Of course, you remember, when you had a small pimple by the side of your nose, you were completely convinced that everyone noticed, and it was the size of a quarter. If you remember what it was to magnify every little thing, you have a clue of what it is like to raise a toddler.

Everything about a toddler is measured and quantified. For example, your child is measured and weighed at their well-baby check-ups. The circumference of his or her head is measured, too. And then, your child is charted against all other children to determine his or her physical development.

Is the nineteenth percentile a good thing?

What about the eighty-eighth?

Does that slight bow-leggedness in your child, who is not even walking yet, mean he's going to grow up and look like a cowboy who's spent the longer part of his day riding bareback?

Robin Williams once did a routine in which he talked about what it's like to be a new parent. He described imagining his child's future and, at first, finding great joy and comfort in imagining his child standing before the Nobel Prize Committee, accepting his prize. But then, you remember Kevin Hart's sketch about his children and a more troubling vision of the future intruded, and you picture your child as an adult, standing across the counter at a fast-food emporium.

"You want fries with that?"

If our child speaks early, we are convinced they are gifted. If they are speaking 'within range,' we comfort ourselves with their 'thoughtfulness.' But if they speak after the'"appropriate' age insistently, we start worrying whether something is 'wrong.'

Few things fill the parents of toddlers with the level of anguish as toilet training. Is the child who is successfully toilet trained at nine months a budding Mozart or someone sure to grow up with all sorts of psychological issues? Is the child who still wears diapers at twenty months troubled or just fine?

These questions are overwhelming and interesting in the abstract, but never minimize the emotion you will pour into each of them and thousands of others. You will take no comfort from the aunt or grandmother who pooh-poohs the rush to toilet train. "No one wears diapers to college," you'll be told.

Trust me; you will gain no solace from the observation.

"She'll talk when she's ready," likewise, will provide you with little to no comfort.

That magnifying glass you internalized as a prepubescent teen is nothing compared to the one you have internalized as a new parent. Every action, every sound, every smile, every attempt to sit, roll over, stand, walk, eat, laugh, cry; every little thing your child does will cause you incalculable joy and unmitigated terror.

You will find yourself sitting with your child, saying, "Mama, mama," hoping your little darling will echo your sounds. When he doesn't, you will feel your heart freeze and a knot form in your stomach. Jill's little girl says "mama" and "dada," and she's four months younger than your child.

You will find yourself lying in bed at night, staring at the ceiling, wondering, "Is there something wrong?"

You will google every piece of advice given after leaving the pediatrician to discuss your concerns. You'll wrack your brain for any early fevers or exposures to any virus that could cause your child harm. Covid-19 immediately comes to mind. Might your child have come in contact with it? Maybe you shouldn't wait until the morning. Perhaps you should wake your child up and rush him to the emergency room.

At the least, you should call your pediatrician's tele-nurse service and see what they think.

Right?

You roll over and shake your husband awake.

"Huh?"

"I'm worried."

"About what now?" he asks groggily.

You dismiss the tone of his "now" and sit up and describe your fear. He wipes the sleep from his eyes and then shakes his head. "Go back to sleep."

"I can't."

"Can we talk about it in the morning?"

"You don't think we should go to the emergency room now?"

He looks at you like you've lost your mind. "Because our baby is sleeping soundly?" he asks in disbelief.

"No," you say, making a face. "Because she's not talking yet. Maybe something is wrong."

Here's what I want you to promise me. I want you to promise me that when that little darling of yours- the one that has kept you up all night worrying because she hadn't uttered a sensible sound; the one who, when she finally begins to speak- you utter a silent prayer of thanks to the Lord for. I want you to promise me that you'll remember how worried you were when your daughter does not shut up for a minute. When every other word is: Why? She will question you: When she wants to go out with boys; when she wants her curfew later and later and later; when she will argue with you for hours about the reason; and when she's trying to explain that it's okay to wear heels like that to school.

"Everybody is wearing them."

"I don't care what other girls do!

When you close your eyes and remember the days when she was an adorable, nearly silent little angel, don't you dare wish that your darling daughter would just be quiet again!

That is all I ask you to promise.

CHAPTER 18

Toddlers

"**M**y brother-in-law used to tease us that our little boy's name was 'No-Bobby-No," Regina said with a smile and shake of her head.

That poor kid couldn't move left or right without us telling him not to get into something or not to touch something."

She was laughing about it now, but for all the sleepless nights and newness of having a brand new baby in the house, taking care of an infant and baby is generally a lot easier than taking care of a toddler. Why? Because an infant is, for the most part, a blob, a passive little person with fairly simple and understandable needs. A toddler, on the other hand, is mischievous, a burst of energy- sometimes too much energy.

As my mom always said, "Little children, little problems. Big children, big problems." As we will see, she was spot on.

When Jennifer moved with her young family to a quiet, suburban cul-de-sac, she was thrilled to find other neighbors with young children. In particular, she was happy to see that her neighbor, Debbie, had a little boy who was only about nine months older than her little boy, Jimmy, who was nine months at the time.

Debbie's little boy, Sammy, was rushing along the sidewalk one day when Jennifer came outside with Jimmy in her arms.

"I can't wait for when Jimmy really starts to walk," she said.

Debbie looked up with an expression of caution on her face. "Don't be in such a hurry," she said solemnly.

Jennifer was surprised by Debbie's reaction. "What do you mean?"

"You'll see," Debbie promised.

She didn't have to be curious for long. Debbie went on to say, "it was a lot easier when I didn't have to chase him up and down the street. And just try to keep him in the shopping cart at the supermarket is like pulling teeth."

All of a sudden, a new and terrifying world seemed to become plain to Jennifer. The adorable little boy that she held in her arms was soon to become a terrorizing toddler! He would have his hands in everything, pulling every pot and pan out of the cupboard (and bang them together!) She would have to latch every cabinet, every drawer. The toilet seats would have to have the special toddler latches.

She was already starting to feel exhausted.

Soon, her little boy (out of the crib and in his first bed!) would be climbing or jumping out of bed, right over the safety rail they'd installed to keep him safe. The first time he did that, Jennifer fully appreciated that his crib had been not just a cute enclosure, a bed for her baby, but a cell that kept him contained. Now, she realized with panic that she could wake up at any time of the night to find him wandering the house!

What could he climb on?

What could he pull down?

Were the knives secured?

And the talking!

When Jimmy began to talk, Jennifer and her husband were so happy; thrilled. Those first words! They recorded them for posterity. They had spent months talking to him, teaching him to say "mama" and "dada" and the more difficult "nana" and "pop-pop" for when her parents visited. Then, after his first words, they waited anxiously for him to be able to string some words together in a simple sentence.

Ah, the glorious milestones!

Jennifer wrote each and every one of them down in Jimmy's baby book. But soon enough, Jennifer understood exactly what Debbie had been talking about. She had spent what seemed like countless hours chasing Jimmy through department stores, horrified that he seemed to always find some display of lingerie to pull down. When she did manage to get him to sit still for more than two seconds, it seemed that he refused to stop.

She didn't know if she could stand to hear the very same 'knock-knock' joke for the thousandth time without screaming. She didn't know whether to be troubled or amused that he laughed hysterically each time he told it. He wanted the same book read to him over and over and over again.

Was that a sign of something seriously wrong, she wondered. He insisted on 'helping' her when she was cleaning up, easily quadrupling the work.

Jennifer absolutely adored Jimmy, but when he was old enough to register in daycare and then school, the very first question she asked was, "How early can I drop him off?" After the first week, the next question was, "How late can I leave him?" Of course, Debbie could have told her, having asked the same questions the year before.

CHAPTER 19

Tough love

Okay, I'm not saying that every child is gifted or that every child makes the Honor Roll. They don't. So I'm not trying to take away the joy and pride that you might feel when your child is named to the Honor Roll at school or when she gets a note home from the teacher with a star on it. That's great stuff!

All I'm suggesting is hold on to those moments to balance the moments when you wonder what happened to your cute, adorable child. Laminate all their awards to remind them of possibilities for days when the drama kicks in, and "it's the end of the world."

Here are some other things you should know if you have small children in school: Every argument she has with another student does not require your mediation.

Children have a wonderful capacity to forgive and forget (so long as parents don't get involved.) Children do not have to color inside the lines. And no matter how much the teacher pushes the point, they don't have to write on the lines, either. (If these things are issues by the time your child is in middle school, then there may be concerns, however.) A scraped knee will heal nicely without a trip to the pediatrician. However, a hug and kiss will aid the healing process remarkably well. This, too, shall pass. Your child will get a school picture each year. Do not feel compelled to buy the super-sized, fancy 'bonus' packet with your child's photograph laminated to a wood-grain, 8x10 frame like a college diploma, along with eighteen 5x7's and 36 wallet-sized copies.

Unless you have a really big family, and you intend to get the same laminated photograph each year for your child and every other child you ever have, I wouldn't recommend it.

But that's just my perspective. The important thing to note here is that there will be a photograph every year. Every child gets one. Every. Single. One!. I am emphasizing that point for a reason.

Like every child gets a photograph every year, the teacher and the school try very hard to make sure every child is praised. If possible, every child gets to be an honored child in something. Arithmetic. Spelling. Reading. Kickball. Cleaning his cubby.

You get the idea.

As exciting as it is to get a certificate praising your child, try not to put too much pressure on them. Sending out announcements on paper with your child's name on it, to "Oh my god, my child's a genius!" is a big difference.

That might be a step too far and one that, in the long run, will do you and your child more harm than good. Let your child be a child with all the good and the bad that entails. There will be many opportunities to cheer your child on (and you should always be on the lookout for these,) just as there will be ample times when your child will need to be encouraged because she hasn't done as well as she could, or tried as well as she might, or be as friendly as she should be.

Being a child is all about learning how to be in the world — how to get along with others, learn new things safely, experience new things, and find things that make you happy. Parents, and all adults, must guide this process with a very light hand, staying out of the way as much as possible. Our children have an excellent way of letting us know when they need us and when they want to try it on their own.

We just have to listen.

This brings me back to 'honors.'

We're at a weird time when everything has to be 'non-competitive.' Children have races, and there are no winners' ribbons, just 'competitor' ribbons. It's good to let kids play to win and to learn how to lose. That's part of life, too. And something that parents have to teach their kids.

Hey, anyone can teach the easy lessons. The reason we're moms is to teach the hard ones with enough love to make it bearable.

CHAPTER 20

"Taxi..."

Go ahead, make fun of minivans. Enjoy it while you can. Because about the time your kids make it to middle school, you are going to take on a new role, one that you may never have envisioned before. You are going to become little more than a glorified taxi driver.

"Take me to the mall."

"I have baseball practice."

"Football at 5:00."

"Can I go to Dee's house?"

"Can you pick up David so we can have a playdate?"

"Working on a school project at Sam's."

"I want McDonald's (or Burger King, or Pizza Hut, or Kentucky Fried Chicken or you fill in the blank.)"

Each and every one of these things, and a thousand more, have something in common- you. More specifically, you behind the wheel driving your child, your children, your children's friends someplace. Most likely in traffic. Most likely, when you have other things to do. Most likely early in the morning or late at night.

All those years, you dedicated to nurturing your child and caring for her, from feeding, guiding, reading to, and singing to her, to bathing, buying her toys. And now you have been reduced to, Driver. Yes, I said it! Driver!

This is still one of the easiest parts of motherhood.

Slowly the teenage years are creeping up.

You sit in the front seat while your daughter and her friends sit in the backseat, gabbing away about the game, school, other kids. You pretend not to listen. But you listen. You want to know what's happening in your daughter's life, but you feel a bit guilty for eavesdropping.

You want to know which friend will no longer be invited out with you and which boy you may have to 'speak' to when you drop her off at school.

Sometimes you join the conversation. Generally, this is greeted enthusiastically.

The minivan becomes like a drama scene from Power.

Worse, even though you're sitting in the front by yourself, you are not in charge of the music. You barely understand the lyrics. Or you pretend not to know the message of the music. They're playing Chris Brown- "Loyal"- and a wall of sound rises from the back of the car, the likes of which you cannot imagine. Deep down, you are jamming and praying simultaneously, hoping they do not understand what Chris Brown is really talking about in the song.

For most of us, the "Chauffeur" stage is horrible. It's true. There's not much to recommend about it; more cons than pros. However, there are a couple of things that every parent who finds herself taxiing her kids should remember, and positively:

1. The reason you are driving is that they are not. When your kids start driving, some things get easier, and life can become simpler. However, the list of things to worry about grows exponentially.

2. If you're smart, you'll find that the car can become your most intimate setting. Sure, it's frustrating when there are a bunch of kids in the back, and you're completely ignored. But the times when you're driving your child to or from somewhere are often the best times to have great conversations with them; to ask them questions that they might even answer; to bond. Soon you will find yourself reminiscing about the awards, the

first time they spoke, the first time they walked, and wondered what happened to them. Here come the teenage years.

CHAPTER 21

Teen Years- Divide and Conquer

Alicia and I were out for a much-needed drink, swapping "war stories" about our teens when I started crying.

"What happened this time?" Alicia asked me with concern and an expression as if to say, 'Girl, it's always something going on with you.'

"What did she do, and how much will it cost you?" she urged, sitting back and crossing her arms.

I told her none of the above. I thought about my mom and how I needed to call her and apologize for everything I put her through in my teenage years.

Today, I sat in my daughter's room, thinking of those beautiful moments we shared- her first dance recital, her first honor's award, her wall of fame, and her school pictures in order from first through eighth.

When she entered high school, she made a declaration to her father and me.

"Mom, Dad, I am not taking any more stupid school pictures."

Her dad and I looked at each other and replied unrehearsed with a harmonious, "No problem."

We often laugh (when I'm not upset with him for one thing or another) how she stormed out in protest to our response.

I thought about the time she was supposed to stay at her friend's house and literally was in another state. Or the time her dad took her to rehabilitation for smoking weed. (She must have thought he was crazy, or better yet, he was following my direction.)

This beautiful little girl became defiant, unpredictable. I felt guilty about my thoughts. I love my little girl, but I didn't like her very much. Sometimes, I didn't want to deal with her.

"I sometimes feel like I wasn't a good mother," I heard myself say out loud to Alicia.

She stopped me before I could say another word.

"Girl, I'm not going to allow you to beat yourself up. Remember my bundle of joy? Now, you know I feel your pain. We can't let these kids run us. I'm tired of dying my gray hair from the stress."

I recalled how Alicia came home early, and Timmy had a girl in the house. Once, she went to a parent-teacher conference and found out Timmy had missed homework for three weeks.

"Were we this bad?"

I laughed when Alicia asked me that.

"Of course, we were. Actually, we were worse!" I admitted. If you thought that my Alicia and I were an emotional, unstable mess, then you should know what it was like for my husband and me. The teen years. Or, as I like to call them, "the years I became an alcoholic." It would be easy to mention the changes adolescents experience during their teen years. Yet, the most incredible event during this time is the transformation of the parents' relationship.

You managed just fine with compromising and deciding on issues that concerned the family, such as budgeting, where to live, whose family to spend the holidays with, what car to purchase, and even where to have your anniversary dinner. But somehow, when it came to raising a teenager, you and your husband were like water and oil. You weren't sure if you wanted to scream at your teenager or your husband for not siding with you.

Oh sure, there are those mothers who shake their heads and glare at their husbands. "He 's your son!" just as there are all those fathers who hide behind their long days at work. "Just take care of it!" (By "it," I believe they are referring to a situation, not the child. But I cannot be one hundred percent certain on that point.)

The simple truth is that teenagers are infuriating. They seem to exist only to challenge every fiber of your being. They bring out the best and the worst in you. At times they make you shake your head and wonder, "Was I ever that young and annoying?" (The short answer is, "Yes." Then you remember I have to take mom out to dinner and apologize.)

Navigating the teenage years will either have you contemplating murder or wishing you had bought a dog instead. It will humble you and everyone involved. For teens, it means managing a social and academic life while worrying about every minor detail of their physical, emotional, and even spiritual well-being. It is up to us, the moms and dads, to help make that navigating successful (Mostly moms.)

It ain't easy. Let me say it again. It ain't easy.

But what is really, really hard is realizing that in negotiating the difficult terrain of teenage-hood, your child has somehow developed into a brilliant tactician. That is, he has figured out the value of "divide and conquers." He has become — often by design, sometimes unwittingly — a genius at dividing you and your husband.

Maybe it begins innocently enough. "Wait until your father gets home." Maybe you just show a bit more sympathy after a punishment. Perhaps you've always been the disciplinarian.

You're stricter. (You hear your son's voice playing in your head, "Dad understands me more.")

Maybe he has some of the traits you fell in love with but hate in your son.

Well, that's fine and good when everyone behaves. But the first sign of ill-behavior and the "knives" come out.

"You've coddled him too much!"

And, of course, you're not going to take that lying down. "You should have spent more time with him. Then he'd listen to you."

"That kid is swimming in your gene pool."

"What's that supposed to mean?"

"Come on. It's obvious..."

In no time, the conversation has ceased to be about your teen. Instead, it's a self-critique of your parenting, your relationship, your trust in one another. You have been 'good cop'd/bad cop'd.'

Parents that figure out how this is going early in their child's teen years are parents who do a better job of getting through those years — for their own sakes as well as for their teen's sake. Remember 'united front.' You can kill each other in the comforts of your bedroom.

When your child is two years old, there are 'mommy and me' classes. Sure, those are great times for you to help transition your child to school, but they are also great times for you to speak with other moms, ask questions, and compare (in a good way.) Too bad, there are no 'mommy and me' classes for teens. As a result, we feel isolated, desperate, alone. And we feel our husbands don't understand. You think to yourself, if he tells me to calm down one more time, I swear.

We lose context.

To make matters worse, inevitably, you will bump into some other parent at the grocery store or the school or someplace, and they will go on and on about how sweet and polite your child is. You smile and thank the person, but in your mind, you're wondering if they're talking about your child or being sarcastic.

Sweet?

Polite?

How many times have you gone out to dinner with your teen and looked across the table at this sullen, sulking, quiet and annoying human being and wondered,

"Why did we bother bringing her along?" Raising a teenager is aggravating. It is terrifying. It is rarely enjoyable (you didn't realize how much you enjoy drinking.) Whatever you do, accept that you are not your child's friend.

You are your child's mother. She needs you to be that.

Be friendly.

Be respectful.

Be firm and fair.

If they make it through the teenage years, there will come a time when you can be friends. But this period of your child's life isn't the time. They need a grown-up to trust. They don't need an oversized peer.

Be there for them.

And be there for each other.

Breathe!

When you are raising a teenager, you have got to communicate with your partner. You have to be on team 'Unity.' At this age, you must think: it's us against them. Your child will do everything imaginable to divide and conquer.

Don't let it happen.

CHAPTER 22

SATs? College Applications?

J ust when you think that you cannot possibly stand another moment with your teen, something changes. The scatterbrained, disrespectful, disorganized, unfocused child you've been dealing with and fighting with and arguing with for years has suddenly begun to focus.

You are this close to leaving her and your husband, and suddenly, like a storm racing through, there's a kind of calm. Your child has begun to settle down. She is thinking about the future. For many, that means college. For others, it might mean work or military service. Whatever it is, they are leaving your house, and you couldn't be happier. (Does that make you a bad mom? The real answer is NO!) It simply means your worry heightens to a different level. Some skills and lessons need to be learned for both mommy and child for that transition to be successful. The mommy-worry never ends. That's right: never. It will always be there.

Now, your child is absolutely committed to having an active role in that transition. You are another voice, along with friends, teachers, and counselors, to try and make it successful.

I couldn't believe it when Toni came home and asked if she could get an SAT tutor. An SAT tutor? This from my little girl who, as best as I could tell, hadn't done a single homework assignment in two years?

I asked her if she was kidding. She wasn't. She was dead serious. I don't know how it got into her system, but she understood that the SAT was important. The other thing she was doing was thinking about which classes she was going to take. Advanced placement. What prerequisites she needed. Was Spanish better than Italian? Should she study Mandarin? Mandarin, really?

My little girl, whose every other word was 'you-know and like,' was thinking about studying Mandarin. She said it would look good on her college applications.

College applications?

So, for two or three years, I had been living with this barely-recognizable child in my home. So many times, I looked at this rude little person and wondered what she'd done with my adorable little girl? Or the complacent, gloomy girl and wondered what happened to the sweet girl who loved Barbies? I would silently pray for the time when these aliens would abandon my home and return to wherever they came from. Then suddenly, I saw the light at the end of the tunnel. I then found myself claiming my child again and smiling.

College.

Suddenly, saying goodbye isn't such a welcome thought. After eighteen years of blood, sweat, and tears (not to mention joy and excitement), your baby is preparing to say, "Goodbye." To hell with her, she's ready, are you ready? Although the last couple of years have been extremely difficult (and I enjoyed drinking more than I care to admit,) the thought of her leaving had me in a tsunami of emotions.

"I tried to convince her to take classes closer to home so that she could live at home," I had told my friend Danielle about Toni's college plans.

"Oh," said Danielle. "That would be good for you. And for her, too, so you know she's alright, at least her first year on her own." But she had her mind made up. She worked so hard the last two years of high school.

I went home that evening and discussed the options with my husband about trying to convince her to take classes closer to home, and my poor husband gave a side-eye look and walked away.

And just like that, we were shopping at Wal-Mart and Target for dorm supplies. Our daughter was on Facebook with her roommates, making all kinds of living arrangement plans. They had already discussed who would get the television for the room, the microwave, the music system, etc. It seemed like they knew everything about each other's lives. It was as though they had known each other their entire lives. They appeared to be like old friends, who hadn't seen each other in years and suddenly wanted to live together.

If your experience with moving your freshman into college is anything like mine was, then it will be traumatic, emotional, and exhausting. Your husband will get sore in places he didn't even know he had, and although he's proud and happy, he is hoping he will get the woman he fell in love with twenty years ago. Because that lunatic lady he's been living with is something else. Lugging boxes and television up flights of stairs is a small token to have peace in the house again.

You'll likely be carrying large bags of clothes and linen. You may be almost too beat to take in the enormity of what's happening. In the blink of an eye, I went from finding out I was pregnant to taking my baby to college. The little girl I had fallen in love with so many years ago was back, and I'd already forgotten the last four years of hell she put me through.

Where did the time go?

You will have a perfectly good script of all the things you want to say before you leave.

"Have fun, but not too much fun. If you drink (please don't drink! And dear God, don't do drugs!) try and drink responsibly. If you leave your drink on a table, do not pick it up. If you go out in a group, come back in a group. Please never get in anyone's car you don't know. And make sure they haven't been drinking.

Come home for the holidays."

You are already thinking of a visiting day.

All the things you want to say before you leave; all the lessons you want to impart. All the things you know you haven't said all the years but wanted to.

And in the end, all you do is cry and cry some more and say I love you about a hundred times.

Meanwhile, your husband cannot believe what he is witnessing. Last year, this time, you were screaming at the top of your lungs about him and 'his' daughter.

CHAPTER 23

A degree in Music Appreciation...

I can't believe I'm yelling again. Guess who graduated and many thousands of dollars later is moving back into her old room, in her twin bed with no real job prospects? No real plans beyond "maybe I'll travel a little."

Really? You think. And who's paying for this little bit of travel?

But the truth is, after getting through graduation (thrilling,) packing up her apartment and moving back, doing twenty-five loads of laundry (you knew you should have taken it all to a Laundromat,) you're just glad to have her home. (Your husband may feel different.) With a couple of piercings and a small tattoo (that you can see. You don't want to know about the ones you can't see,) a streak of blonde through her dark hair, she doesn't look totally different. She's got portfolios of artwork she's done, along with books, and more books, and a little more books. You have no idea where she'll put it all, but she assures you it will be fine stacked in her room until she gets settled and finds a place.

Find a place? Really? With what money? But the first few nights are amazing. You make her favorite meals. She hangs out with you, watching your favorite television shows. You watch some home movies of when she was a little girl, and you delight in how she giggles at herself and calls herself "cute."

You think it's funny that she can't believe she was ever that small. You can't believe that she's not that small anymore!

There is a moment when you think, "Hey, this is kind of nice." But then your daughter is in touch with some other friends who are back. They go out, and she doesn't come home until 3:00 in the morning.

Three in the morning! Oh no!

You wake your husband to complain about her coming in at 3:00 A.M.

He tells you to go to sleep and says, "it's not that serious." The next morning you are too upset to say good morning to your husband.

You pace in the kitchen back and forth until she finally wakes up.

"But that's what college kids do," she explains when she gets up at noon the following day. "It's no big deal."

No big deal? Not while you're living under my roof!

Suddenly, it's like high school again. Only now, she really is an adult. This is crazy. She is calmer and makes more sense than you.

When are you going to find a job?

"Come on," she says. "I only graduated last month. It's summer."

No, you want to tell her. It's not summer. It's life.

But you don't. Not yet. Somehow you fear that if you push too hard, you will lose her, and you don't want that.

Gradually, just like the last couple of years of high school, she gets focused. Friends are going to work. Some are going to graduate or professional school. A couple of friends are leaving for the service.

It's time to face life. She gets a job. Not a great job, but a job. After all, what is a degree in Art Appreciation going to do career-wise? She talks about going to school to teach, to become a nurse, maybe work with children. Meanwhile, she has a job in an office.

Then she is promoted to office manager. Wow, that was fast. You're proud of her, (but you think to yourself: is this what I paid for?) She's making enough money now to get an apartment, which she shares with a couple of other young women (young women!) who work in her office or offices nearby.

You speak to her every day.

Then once a week.

She tells you about the office- the office politics. The people she works with, she sounds good. She mentions another professional in the building. Jeffrey. "Nice guy," she says. They've gone out a couple of times. Nothing serious.

"No, mom. Everything's good," she says when you push a bit on the matter.

You find a way to ask about Jeffrey when you talk to her.

"Stop," she says.

"Am I going to meet him?"

"Maybe," she says. "It's not that big a deal," she adds.

It doesn't stop her from crying to you when she is having a disagreement with him—you counsel patience. "Men get scared easily," you say, although you have no idea what you're trying to accomplish by saying it, other than trying to make her feel better. It seems to work.

Too well. A month later, she's bringing Jeffrey to meet you and her dad. He looks like a nice guy. You can see why she likes him. They're both so young, you think to yourself as you sit across the table from them. Which is the reason you are completely unprepared for them to announce that they're getting married.

Married! What in the world? Your husband grabs your hand, and he can tell the lunatic lady is back. You're too busy trying to slow the pounding of your heart to see just how happy and excited she is. A wedding? You're not at all ready.

That night, you don't sleep, which means your husband doesn't sleep. You bombard him in a rant of questions and comments in a one-way conversation.

"Why are they rushing?"

"The first time we meet him, they announce they're getting married."

"What's wrong with her?"

"She doesn't even know him; he could be a serial killer."

"It's your fault. You spoiled her."

"I don't like him!"

Your husband listens silently, afraid to voice an opinion or a thought.

You finally turn to him and say," You don't have anything to say?"

He looks at you again in disbelief and turns over, and tries to fall asleep.

Meanwhile, your mind and heart are racing. You are frantic, and you cannot believe she didn't have the courtesy to prepare you (you remind yourself that a child is composed of two DNAs.)

You finally fall asleep around 4:00 A.M

CHAPTER 24

The Cycle of Life

Reluctantly you plan her wedding. You made an agreement with your husband to keep your thoughts and opinions to yourself. And he promised to listen patiently.

The wedding was beautiful.

You cried. Your husband, the big tough guy, had tears running down his cheeks as he danced with his little girl. Now she's married and off on her own life.

It's all good. (You hope.)

You're not exactly prepared, on Monday morning, when the phone rings.

"Hello?"

"Hi, mom."

"Hi, baby. What's up? Aren't you at work?"

"Mom, I'm pregnant!".

Good thing you're sitting down.

After the initial shock, you smile, look-up to the sky, and simply ask that your daughter is blessed with a baby girl so that she can experience every emotion you feel for her and every emotion she made you feel.

A NOTE FROM THE AUTHOR:

I truly appreciate your love and support as I continue to embark on my next journey in this thing called life. As in my first book, I Have A Purpose, I wrote it from the heart.

When I wrote this book, I tapped into my own experience and that of others. Admitting we are IMPERFECTLY PERFECT allows us to release some of the pressure we put on ourselves, including the stress from our families and society. Our skin tones may be different, our appearance may change or be different, but WE all want the same thing: an honest, loving, and respectful relationship with our husband and parents. We want our children to be a better version of ourselves.

We are all given a purpose in life. Life is never perfect and definitely not always good. But one thing that always remains true to our core is that we have a purpose.

We must never forget to laugh. Don't take yourself so seriously. Find something to enjoy and positivity in whatever you do.

Remember, perfect only applies to the love you strive to achieve...we all are Imperfectly Perfect...

Purposeful,
Carmen Ashe

Ladies:

Our actions are sometimes hilarious and scary at times. Stop speaking to your man with such disrespect and disregard and treating him like he's your child. He is a man. Let him be one. Remember why you fell in love with him.

Men:

We are not perfect, but neither are you! Stop expecting a woman to look a certain way, act a certain way, or cater to your every unreasonable desire. When you make a commitment, make sure you understand what those conditions entail. Please don't play with her emotions.

Ladies and Men:

Sometimes, no matter how hard you try or how much you try to love someone, the relationship may not always work out. And that's okay; walk away. However, be mindful to not walk away from your children, as they are innocent and still want your presence and need your love.

To learn about the Author,

Visit: www.Ihaveapurpose.com

ACKNOWLEDGMENT

To ALL the AMAZING Women in my life - especially Pat, Ginger, my bestie Marcia a.k.a. "Mira," my sistas Kisha, Mishea a.k.a. "Shea," last but not least Verlie Lloyd a.k.a. Momma. I love you all.

To the women who came into my life for a reason or a season- Thank you.

To all the men- On behalf of the women: Thank you for being patient, understanding, and sometimes accepting our crazy moments.

To the artists who sacrificed their lives to follow 'the dream,' - your music has helped many through the happiest and darkest times. I would especially like to thank - Patti Labelle, Gladys Knight, Anita Baker, Carol King, Faith Hill, Shaina Twain, Yolanda Adams, CeCe Winans, Tina Turner, Stephanie Mills, Mariah Carey, Monica, Faith, Martina McBride, Regina Bell, Mikki Howard, and last but certainly not least the late great Whitney Houston.

To my beautiful Nieces- Never dim your lights. YOU ARE BEAUTIFUL. YOU ARE ENOUGH. I love you all.

To my Purpose: Ellie and Tony *If I Could*

To my Grands- Nyla, Roclyn, Trey, and now Isla there are no words that can describe how my heart feels each and every time I see you, love you all with my heart and soul.

My number #1 fan, (my late husband,) as I look back at our relationship, all I can do is smile and laugh. Through the years, I wondered how you managed with me (lol.) When I doubted myself, felt unpretty, and questioned my actions, you brought me back to reality. You had patience, understanding, and unforgettable love that carries me to this date. You were brutally honest, which is one of the many things that I miss most about you. (Ironically, your son has that trait as well, which I love and hate at the same time.) I recently found a card you gave me in 1997. It read: I've always thought of our life together as a great love story written by a truly great Author- You know who that Author is? Thank you for loving and believing in me. I love you always...Until we meet again.

ABOUT THE AUTHOR

Understanding the extent of pressure women face daily, Carmen narrates from the minds of women, detailing the sacrifices we make for our relationships, our children, and ourselves. She brilliantly incorporates her love for music into these funny but realistic emotions expressed by women.

In her debut book, *I Have a Purpose,* Carmen sacrificed her vulnerability to share her personal journey for finding happiness after a series of unfortunate life-changing events. She surrendered her humility to allow herself to tell such a heartfelt and intimate story so that it could help others.

Now, Carmen continues to help others by lending her voice to the speechless and representing those who may not be able to assert their presence. Children are also very important to Carmen. She proudly and passionately teaches students the principles of mindfulness beyond the academic walls of New York City public schools. It has always been necessary for Carmen to reach the youth at an impressionable time in their lives to instill a sense of purpose in them early on.

In *Imperfectly Perfect,* Carmen aspires to influence others to find their purpose while learning to manage the unavoidable and the avoidable ins and outs of life. She hopes that this book will positively impact those who read it as her first book was as healing to write.

TikTok Marketing
for Dentists: No Dancing Involved!

Josh Rimmington
2023

TikTok Marketing for Dentists: No Dancing Involved!

Chapters:

1. Chapter 1 The Power of TikTok Marketing.............. 5
2. Chapter 2 Understanding Your Dental Audience .. 13
3. Chapter 3 Crafting Compelling Content: Beyond the Drill 23
4. Chapter 4 Navigating TikTok's Features for Dental Marketing.. 34
5. Chapter 5 Hashtags and Trends: Making Your Mark 44
6. Chapter 6 Building Your TikTok Brand as a Dentist 52
7. Chapter 7 Educating and Entertaining: Finding the Balance 62
8. Chapter 8 Collaborations and Influencer Partnerships 72
9. Chapter 9 Going Viral: Strategies for Maximum Reach.. 81
10. Chapter 10 Measuring Success: Analytics and Insights 92
11. Chapter 11 Overcoming Challenges in Dental TikTok Marketing... 101
12. Chapter 12 Avoiding Common Mistakes: Lessons Learned 112
13. Chapter 13 Keeping Up with TikTok Trends....... 122
14. Chapter 14 Beyond TikTok: Integrating with Your Overall Marketing 130
15. Chapter 15 Sustaining Your TikTok Presence: Longevity in Dental Marketing............................. 141

Chapter 1
The Power of TikTok Marketing

"The power of TikTok marketing lies in its ability to turn viewers into participants, and participants into loyal advocates of your dental practice."

In the ever-evolving landscape of digital marketing, TikTok has emerged as a force to be reckoned with. What began as a platform primarily for entertainment and dance videos has quickly evolved into a versatile tool for businesses and professionals to connect with their audience in unique and engaging ways. As a dentist, you might wonder how a platform known for viral dances and lip-syncing can possibly be relevant to your practice. In this chapter, we'll explore the transformative power of TikTok marketing for dentists and why it's a game-changer in the world of dental marketing.

TikTok: More Than Dance Moves

TikTok's journey from a teenage phenomenon to a marketing powerhouse is nothing short of remarkable. With over a billion active users worldwide, it has become one of the most influential social media platforms. What sets TikTok apart is its ability to capture attention quickly. The platform's short-form videos, typically ranging from 15 to 60 seconds, are designed to be concise, engaging, and memorable.

For dentists, this format offers a golden opportunity. In a world where attention spans are dwindling, TikTok provides a platform where you can deliver valuable content in bite-sized, easily digestible portions. It's the ideal space to educate your audience about oral health, demystify dental procedures, and address common concerns—all while keeping viewers entertained.

The Visual Power of TikTok

They say a picture is worth a thousand words, and on TikTok, a video can be worth millions of impressions. The platform's emphasis on visual content allows you to showcase your expertise like never before. Whether you're demonstrating proper brushing techniques, explaining the benefits of orthodontic treatment, or sharing before-and-after transformations, TikTok's video format allows you to illustrate your message vividly.

As a dentist, your work is inherently visual. Patients want to see the results of your procedures, understand the techniques you employ, and visualize the improvements you can make to their oral health. TikTok lets you do all of this in a format that's not only informative but also captivating.

Building Trust through Authenticity

One of TikTok's most compelling features is its authenticity. Users are drawn to content that feels genuine and relatable. As a dentist, you have the opportunity to humanize your practice and connect with patients on a personal level. Share behind-the-scenes glimpses of your clinic, introduce your team, and showcase your commitment to patient care.

Authenticity breeds trust, and trust is a cornerstone of successful dental marketing. When viewers see the face behind the dental chair, when they witness your passion for oral health, and when they hear you address their concerns with empathy, they are more likely to trust you with their dental care. TikTok offers a stage to build this trust in a way that feels natural and unforced.

Captivating the Next Generation

Dental marketing isn't just about attracting current patients; it's also about reaching the next generation of dental care seekers. TikTok is particularly popular among younger demographics, including teenagers and young adults. These individuals are not just the patients of today but also the lifelong patients you aim to cultivate.

By establishing a presence on TikTok, you're speaking the language of the future. You're meeting your potential patients where they are, in a space they're comfortable with. You're providing them with valuable information about oral health that can shape their lifelong habits. You're becoming their go-to source of dental knowledge, even before they step into a dental office.

The Viral Potential

One of the most exciting aspects of TikTok marketing is its viral potential. A well-crafted video can quickly gain momentum, reaching thousands, or even millions, of viewers in a matter of hours. Virality is not only about amassing views; it's also about sparking conversations and engagements.

Imagine a video where you address a common dental myth, debunk it with scientific evidence, and offer a practical tip for maintaining healthy teeth. If this video resonates with viewers, they'll not only watch it but also like, comment, and share it with their followers. In the world of TikTok, this ripple effect can result in your content spreading far and wide.

Educate and Entertain: The Winning Formula

At its core, TikTok marketing for dentists is about blending education with entertainment. It's about delivering informative content in a way that captivates and engages. It's about taking your knowledge and packaging it in a format that's as enjoyable as it is enlightening.

In the chapters that follow, we'll delve deeper into the strategies and techniques that will help you master this winning formula. You'll learn how to craft compelling content, understand your dental audience, navigate TikTok's features, harness the power of hashtags and trends, and build a TikTok brand that resonates with authenticity.

But before we dive into the specifics, take a moment to appreciate the power of TikTok marketing. It's a tool that can transform your dental practice's online presence, connect you with a new generation of patients, and position you as a trusted voice in oral health. The journey ahead is exciting, and the possibilities are boundless. Get ready to embark on a TikTok adventure where no dancing is involved, but the impact is profound.

Chapter 2
Understanding Your Dental Audience

"To craft content that resonates, you must first understand your audience's dental desires, fears, and aspirations."

In the world of TikTok marketing for dentists, understanding your audience is the compass that guides your content strategy. Your audience isn't a monolithic entity; it's a diverse group of individuals with varying needs, preferences, and expectations. To effectively connect with them, you must first understand them. In this chapter, we'll delve into the intricacies of comprehending your dental audience on TikTok.

The Demographic Mosaic

TikTok boasts a wide-ranging user base, but when it comes to dental marketing, demographics can play a crucial role. Begin by dissecting your audience's age groups, as different generations have distinct oral health needs.

For example, younger viewers may be more interested in content about braces, teeth whitening, and general oral hygiene. Older viewers might be looking for information on dental implants, gum disease prevention, and denture care. Tailoring your content to these age-specific interests can help you connect more effectively.

Addressing Dental Anxiety

Dental anxiety is a common concern among patients. Many people dread dental appointments due to fear of pain, discomfort, or simply not knowing what to expect. TikTok provides an ideal platform to address these fears and misconceptions.

Consider creating content that demystifies dental procedures, explains pain management techniques, or shares patient testimonials highlighting their positive experiences. By addressing these concerns, you're not only educating your audience but also positioning your practice as empathetic and patient-focused.

Beyond Basic Dental Care

While basic oral hygiene is a universal topic, your audience's interests likely extend beyond that. TikTok allows you to explore a wide array of dental-related subjects. Some viewers might be curious about cosmetic dentistry, while others may want to learn about the latest advancements in orthodontics or restorative procedures.

Understanding these nuanced interests within your audience allows you to diversify your content and cater to specific niches. This targeted approach can help you attract viewers who are genuinely interested in the services you offer.

Cultural Sensitivity and Inclusivity

In today's globalized world, your dental audience may consist of individuals from diverse cultural backgrounds. It's crucial to be culturally sensitive and inclusive in your content. Avoid assumptions and stereotypes, and ensure your messaging resonates with a broad spectrum of viewers.

Consider addressing oral health practices and traditions from various cultures. This not only showcases your awareness but also demonstrates your commitment to providing inclusive dental care.

Feedback and Engagement

Engagement isn't a one-way street. While you're creating content to engage your audience, you should also actively seek their feedback and input. Encourage viewers to comment, ask questions, and share their dental experiences.

Monitor the comments section of your videos diligently. Respond to queries promptly, provide informative answers, and address concerns with empathy. Engaging with your audience fosters a sense of community and trust, which are invaluable in building long-term patient relationships.

Analytics as a Compass

TikTok provides a treasure trove of analytics and insights that can offer a deeper understanding of your audience. These metrics can reveal viewer demographics, engagement rates, and which types of content resonate most.

Regularly reviewing TikTok's analytics can guide your content strategy. If you notice that videos about a particular dental topic garner more views and engagement, consider creating more content around that subject.

The Power of Polls and Surveys

Another effective way to understand your audience is by using TikTok's polling and survey features. You can create interactive content that allows viewers to vote on topics they'd like to see, ask them about their dental concerns, or even run dental-related challenges.

Polls and surveys not only provide valuable insights but also engage your audience actively in shaping your content. It's a win-win approach that strengthens your connection with viewers.

Building Personas

Creating audience personas can be a powerful strategy. Personas are fictional representations of your ideal viewers, complete with characteristics, interests, and pain points. By developing personas, you can tailor your content to speak directly to these imagined individuals, making your messaging more relevant and relatable.

For example, you might create personas like "Sarah, the Braces Enthusiast," or "Mark, the Oral Health Novice." These personas guide your content creation process, ensuring that you consistently address the needs and interests of your diverse audience.

Understanding your dental audience on TikTok is an ongoing journey. It requires active listening, data analysis, and a commitment to adapt to changing preferences and trends. In the chapters that follow, we'll explore how to craft compelling content that resonates with your audience, keeping them engaged and informed on their journey to better oral health.

Chapter 3
Crafting Compelling Content: Beyond the Drill

"Creating compelling TikTok content is like sculpting smiles – it requires artistry, precision, and a touch of magic."

In the world of TikTok marketing for dentists, content is the crown jewel. It's not enough to simply have a presence on the platform; you must create content that captivates, educates, and resonates with your dental audience. This chapter delves into the art of crafting compelling TikTok content that goes beyond the dental drill and leaves a lasting impression.

The Magic of Storytelling

At the heart of compelling content lies storytelling. Stories have a unique power to engage emotions, convey information, and create memorable experiences. As a dentist, you have a wealth of stories to tell—patient success stories, transformational journeys, and the daily life of your practice.

Consider sharing before-and-after visuals with narratives of patients who have undergone remarkable dental transformations under your care. Highlight their journeys, struggles, and newfound confidence. Storytelling humanizes your practice and connects viewers on a personal level.

Educational Nuggets

TikTok is a treasure trove of educational opportunities. Your content should aim to enlighten viewers about oral health, demystify dental procedures, and provide practical tips for maintaining healthy teeth and gums. But remember, TikTok's format is short and snappy, so keep your educational content concise and engaging.

For instance, create short videos on topics like "The Importance of Flossing," "How to Choose the Right Toothbrush," or "Five Foods for Stronger Teeth." These bite-sized educational nuggets empower viewers with valuable information.

Behind-the-Scenes Glimpses

TikTok allows you to pull back the curtain and offer viewers a behind-the-scenes look at your dental practice. Showcasing your clinic's daily operations, introducing your team, and providing insights into your commitment to patient care humanizes your brand and fosters trust.

Consider creating a "Day in the Life of a Dentist" series or spotlighting your dental hygienists, receptionists, and dental assistants. These glimpses into your practice not only make you more relatable but also create a sense of familiarity among viewers.

Myth-Busting and Facts

The world of dentistry is riddled with myths and misconceptions. Use TikTok to debunk these myths with scientific facts and evidence-based information. Address common dental concerns, such as the fear of dental procedures, the truth about fluoride, or the reality of dental pain management.

Myth-busting content not only educates but also positions you as a trusted source of accurate information. It's an excellent way to dispel fears and uncertainties that might be preventing potential patients from seeking dental care.

Interactive Challenges and Quizzes

Engagement is the lifeblood of TikTok. Create interactive challenges and quizzes that encourage viewers to participate and test their dental knowledge. For example, you could launch a "Brushing Challenge" where viewers demonstrate their toothbrushing techniques or a "Dental Trivia Quiz" to test their oral health knowledge.

These interactive elements not only boost engagement but also foster a sense of community and competition among your viewers.

Patient Testimonials

There's no stronger endorsement than a satisfied patient sharing their success story. Encourage patients to provide video testimonials about their experiences with your practice. These authentic stories speak volumes about your expertise and patient care.

Ensure that the testimonials highlight the transformational aspects of their dental journey. Whether it's a smile makeover, orthodontic treatment, or painless tooth extraction, these stories can inspire and reassure potential patients.

Collaborations and Expert Insights

Collaborations with other TikTok creators or dental experts can inject diversity and fresh perspectives into your content. Partner with influencers in the dental or healthcare niche to create joint videos or seek expert insights on specific dental topics.

Collaborations not only expand your reach but also expose your audience to different viewpoints and expertise. They can also be a source of inspiration and creativity for your content.

The Power of Visuals

TikTok is a visual platform, and your content should leverage this aspect to the fullest. Use striking visuals to illustrate your points, whether it's animated diagrams explaining dental procedures or captivating visuals of dental transformations.

Consider utilizing visual effects and overlays to add a touch of creativity to your videos. The more visually appealing your content, the more likely it is to capture and retain viewers' attention.

Consistency Is Key

Consistency is the backbone of successful TikTok marketing. Develop a content calendar that outlines when and what type of content you'll post. Consistent posting not only keeps your audience engaged but also signals reliability and commitment.

Remember that TikTok's algorithm rewards consistency. The more you post, the more likely your content is to be featured on viewers' "For You" pages, increasing your reach.

Engage and Respond

The conversation doesn't end with your video. Actively engage with viewers by responding to comments, answering questions, and fostering dialogue. Engagement transforms one-time viewers into a loyal community.

Monitoring the comments section also provides valuable insights into your audience's needs and concerns, which can inform future content.

In the chapters that follow, we'll explore how to navigate TikTok's features, harness the power of hashtags and trends, build your TikTok brand, and measure the success of your dental marketing efforts. Crafting compelling content is just the beginning of your TikTok journey, but it's a crucial foundation for building a thriving presence on the platform.

Chapter 4
Navigating TikTok's Features for Dental Marketing

"TikTok's features are your compass; use them wisely to navigate the vast seas of dental marketing."

TikTok isn't just about creating and posting videos; it's a dynamic platform with a plethora of features designed to enhance your content and engage your audience. In this chapter, we'll explore the key features of TikTok and how to navigate them effectively for dental marketing.

The Basics: Creating Your Account

Before you can dive into TikTok's features, you'll need to set up your professional account. If you haven't already, here's how:

Download the TikTok App: Start by downloading the TikTok app from your device's app store.

- **Sign Up:** Launch the app and sign up using your email or phone number. You can also sign up using an existing social media account like Facebook or Google.

- **Switch to a Pro Account:** Once your account is created, switch to a "Pro Account." This gives you access to analytics and insights, which are invaluable for understanding your audience.

Navigating the Home Feed

TikTok's home feed is where you'll discover content from creators you follow and recommendations tailored to your interests. Here's how to make the most of it:

- **Following Relevant Creators:** Follow dental professionals, oral health experts, and influencers in your niche to stay updated on industry trends and gather inspiration for your own content.
- **Engaging with Content:** Like, comment on, and share content that resonates with you. Engagement not only fosters community but can also lead to your content being recommended to others.
- **Discovering Trends:** Pay attention to trending hashtags and challenges related to dentistry. Participating in relevant trends can boost your visibility.

Crafting Compelling Content

Creating content on TikTok is at the heart of your dental marketing strategy. Here are some tips:

- **Video Creation:** Tap the '+' button at the bottom center of your screen to start creating a video. You can record clips in segments, add music, and incorporate visual effects to make your content visually appealing.

- **Duration:** TikTok videos are typically short, ranging from 15 to 60 seconds. Keep your content concise and engaging to retain viewers' attention.

- **Captions and Hashtags:** Write informative captions that provide context for your video. Use relevant hashtags to increase the discoverability of your content. For dental marketing, consider using tags like #OralHealth, #DentalTips, or #SmileMakeover.

- **Engage Your Audience:** Encourage viewers to like, comment, share, and follow your account. Pose questions, ask for opinions, and foster interaction in the comments section.

- **Visual Appeal:** Leverage TikTok's editing tools to enhance your video's visual appeal. You can add captions, stickers, filters, and even draw on your videos to emphasize key points.

Embracing TikTok Challenges

Challenges are a major part of TikTok's culture. They're user-generated trends that encourage others to participate. Engaging with challenges can help your content gain visibility. Here's how:

- **Participate Actively:** Join dental-related challenges that align with your content. For example, if there's a "Brushing Challenge," create a video showcasing proper brushing techniques.

- **Create Your Own Challenge:** Consider launching your dental challenge. This can help you establish authority in your niche and encourage others to create content related to your challenge.

Leveraging TikTok's Live Feature

TikTok Live allows you to broadcast in real-time, interact with your audience, and answer questions on the spot. Here's how to use it:

- **Plan Your Live Session:** Schedule your live session in advance and promote it on your TikTok account. This gives your audience time to prepare questions and engage with your live stream.

- **Engage Actively:** During the live session, interact with viewers by responding to their comments and questions. Encourage them to like and share your live stream to reach a wider audience.

Utilizing TikTok Ads

TikTok offers advertising options that can help you reach a broader audience. While this often involves a budget, it can be an effective way to promote your dental practice. TikTok ads include:

- **In-Feed Ads:** These appear as native content in users' feeds, much like regular TikTok videos. You can create engaging ads with a call to action.

- **Branded Hashtag Challenges:** Collaborate with TikTok to create sponsored hashtag challenges that encourage user-generated content related to your brand.

- **Branded Effects:** Create your own special effects, stickers, or filters that users can apply to their videos.

Measuring Success with TikTok Analytics

TikTok provides analytics and insights that help you understand your audience and the performance of your content. Here's how to access and use them:

- **Access Insights:** Go to your TikTok profile, tap the three dots in the upper right corner, and select "Analytics."
- **Audience Insights:** Understand your follower demographics, including age, gender, and location. Use this information to tailor your content to your audience.
- **Content Insights:** Review the performance of your videos, including views, likes, comments, and shares. Identify which content resonates most with your audience and create more of it.

Navigating TikTok's features for dental marketing requires a combination of creativity, strategy, and a deep understanding of your audience. In the chapters that follow, we'll explore specific strategies for using TikTok's features to your advantage, including harnessing the power of hashtags and trends, building your TikTok brand, and measuring the success of your dental marketing efforts.

Chapter 5
Hashtags and Trends: Making Your Mark

"In the world of TikTok, hashtags and trends are your brushstrokes on the canvas of discovery."

In the vibrant world of TikTok marketing for dentists, staying relevant and visible is paramount. Hashtags and trends are your tickets to achieving just that. In this chapter, we'll explore how to leverage these powerful tools to make your mark on TikTok and reach a wider audience.

The Power of Hashtags

Hashtags are the bread and butter of TikTok. They categorize your content, making it discoverable to users interested in specific topics. Here's how to wield hashtags effectively:

- **Choose Relevant Hashtags:** Select hashtags that directly relate to your dental content. For example, if you're sharing tips on braces care, use tags like #BracesTips or #Orthodontics.
- **Mix Broad and Niche Hashtags:** Incorporate a mix of widely used hashtags and more niche ones. While popular hashtags can expose your content to a larger audience, niche tags help you connect with viewers genuinely interested in your content.
- **Create Your Own Branded Hashtag:** Consider crafting a unique hashtag for your dental practice. It can serve as your brand's signature and encourage viewers to engage with your content. Promote it consistently in your videos and captions.
- **Monitor Trending Hashtags:** Keep an eye on trending hashtags in the dental and healthcare niches. Participating in relevant trends can boost your content's visibility. Joining a trending challenge can

put your video in front of thousands or even millions of viewers.

- **Limit the Number of Hashtags:** TikTok recommends using 3-5 hashtags per video for optimal visibility. Using too many can make your content appear spammy.

Riding the Trend Wave

Trends are the lifeblood of TikTok. They're viral challenges, dances, and concepts that capture the platform's attention. Here's how to ride the trend wave effectively:

- **Stay Informed:** Keep a close watch on trending challenges and themes within the TikTok community. The "Discover" page on the app often highlights trending content.

- **Participate Actively:** If a trend aligns with your content and brand, don't hesitate to participate. Create your take on the trend, infusing it with your dental expertise. Remember, adding value to trends is key.

- **Inject Creativity:** Put your unique spin on a trend to stand out. For example, if there's a popular dance challenge, incorporate dental props or educational messages into your dance routine.

- **Time Sensitivity:** Trends come and go quickly on TikTok. Jump on them while they're hot to maximize your visibility. Freshness is vital in the fast-paced world of TikTok.

Crafting Trend-Related Content

When participating in trends, it's essential to create content that seamlessly integrates with the theme while staying true to your dental expertise:

- **Educational Trends:** If a trend involves educating viewers, seize the opportunity. For instance, if there's a trend about "Life Hacks," create dental life hacks that help viewers improve their oral health.

- **Challenges with a Twist:** Put a dental twist on popular challenges. For example, if there's a fitness challenge, adapt it to "Dental Fitness" by sharing exercises that strengthen jaw muscles.

- **Inspirational Stories:** If a trend revolves around personal stories or transformations, showcase dental success stories from your practice. Highlight before-and-after transformations and patient testimonials.

- **Behind-the-Scenes:** Share behind-the-scenes glimpses of your clinic while incorporating trending themes. This humanizes your practice and makes it more relatable.

Measuring the Impact

TikTok provides insights into how your content performs with specific hashtags and trends. Here's how to measure their impact:

- **Analytics:** Use TikTok's analytics to track the performance of videos associated with particular hashtags. Identify which hashtags generate the most views, likes, comments, and shares.

- **Engagement:** Monitor the engagement on your trend-related videos. Are viewers actively participating in the trend by liking, commenting, and sharing? This indicates the effectiveness of your content.

- **Follower Growth:** Keep an eye on your follower count when you engage in trends. If your content resonates with viewers, you're likely to see an increase in followers.

- **Collaborations:** Explore collaboration opportunities with TikTok creators who excel in trend-related content. Partnering with trendsetters can amplify your reach.

Trend Responsibly

While riding the trend wave can be highly effective, it's essential to do so responsibly:

- **Relevance:** Ensure that the trend aligns with your content and messaging. Irrelevant participation can confuse your audience.
- **Authenticity:** Stay true to your dental expertise and values. Don't compromise professionalism for the sake of trends.
- **Ethical Considerations:** Be mindful of any challenges or trends that may promote harmful practices or go against ethical guidelines.

Hashtags and trends are the dynamic pulse of TikTok. When used strategically, they can propel your dental marketing efforts to new heights, exposing your content to a broader audience and solidifying your position as a trusted voice in oral health. In the chapters that follow, we'll continue to explore ways to build your TikTok brand, engage with your audience, and measure the success of your dental marketing efforts.

Chapter 6
Building Your TikTok Brand as a Dentist

"Your TikTok brand isn't just a logo; it's the trust you build, the knowledge you share, and the smiles you create."

In the world of TikTok, your brand is more than just a logo or a name—it's the essence of your dental practice. Building a strong brand presence on TikTok can help you connect with your audience, establish trust, and stand out in a crowded digital landscape. In this chapter, we'll explore the steps to build your TikTok brand as a dentist.

Define Your Brand Identity

Your brand identity encompasses your values, personality, and the unique qualities that set your dental practice apart. Start by defining your brand identity:

- **Mission and Values:** What values drive your practice? Is it a commitment to patient comfort, excellence in dental care, or a focus on community health? Define your mission and core values.
- **Personality:** How do you want your brand to be perceived? Are you friendly and approachable, or professional and authoritative? Your brand's personality should align with your target audience.
- **Unique Selling Proposition (USP):** What makes your practice unique? It could be cutting-edge technology, a particular approach to patient care, or a specialisation in a specific area of dentistry.

Consistency is Key

Consistency is the cornerstone of brand building. Ensure that your TikTok content aligns with your brand identity:

- **Visual Branding:** Use consistent visuals, including your logo, colour scheme, and typography, in your profile picture, banners, and video overlays.
- **Tone of Voice:** Maintain a consistent tone of voice in your captions and narration. Whether it's informative, friendly, or professional, your tone should reflect your brand personality.
- **Content Themes:** Develop content themes that are in line with your brand values and expertise. For instance, if your practice is known for cosmetic dentistry, create content that highlights smile transformations.

Tell Your Brand Story

Your brand story is a powerful tool for connecting with your audience. Share the journey of your dental practice:

- **Origin Story:** Tell the story of how your practice came into existence. Highlight any unique challenges or milestones along the way.

- **Team Showcase:** Introduce your dental team to your audience. Share their qualifications, experience, and commitment to patient care.

- **Patient Success Stories:** Showcase before-and-after transformations, along with patient testimonials. Share stories of how your practice has positively impacted lives.

Engage and Interact

Building a brand on TikTok goes beyond one-way communication. Engage actively with your audience:

- **Respond to Comments:** Take the time to respond to comments on your videos. Address questions, offer additional information, and express gratitude for engagement.
- **Host Q&A Sessions:** Conduct live Q&A sessions where viewers can ask dental-related questions. This positions you as a trusted source of information.
- **Acknowledge Milestones:** Celebrate your TikTok milestones with your audience. Whether it's reaching a certain number of followers or an anniversary for your practice, share the joy.

Collaborate and Network

Collaborations can expand your reach and introduce your brand to new audiences:

- **Collaborate with Influencers:** Partner with TikTok influencers in the healthcare or dental niche. Their endorsement can lend credibility to your brand.
- **Cross-Promote:** Collaborate with other dentists or healthcare professionals to cross-promote each other's content.
- **Engage with Industry Associations:** Join dental associations and participate in discussions. Share insights and build relationships with peers in your industry.

Educate and Empower

One of the most effective ways to build your brand as a dentist is by educating and empowering your audience:

- **Educational Content:** Create content that imparts dental knowledge, addresses common concerns, and provides tips for oral health.

- **Empowerment Through Knowledge:** Empower your audience by helping them make informed decisions about their dental care.

- **Highlight Expertise:** Showcase your expertise through detailed explanations of dental procedures, treatment options, and innovations in the field.

Consistent Posting Schedule

Consistency is not only about branding but also about maintaining audience engagement:

- **Posting Schedule:** Develop a regular posting schedule. Whether it's daily, weekly, or biweekly, consistency keeps your audience coming back for more.
- **Variety of Content:** Offer a variety of content, including educational videos, behind-the-scenes glimpses, patient testimonials, and trend-related content.
- **Quality Over Quantity:** While consistency is vital, never compromise on the quality of your content. High-quality, informative videos reflect positively on your brand.

Measure Brand Success

To gauge the success of your brand-building efforts on TikTok:

- **Analytics:** Use TikTok's analytics to track video performance, follower growth, and audience demographics.
- **Audience Feedback:** Pay attention to comments, likes, shares, and the sentiment of your audience. Positive feedback indicates a strong brand connection.
- **Return on Investment (ROI):** Assess the return on investment for any sponsored posts or advertising campaigns.

Building your TikTok brand as a dentist is an ongoing journey. It requires dedication, authenticity, and a genuine commitment to your audience's oral health. As you continue to engage, educate, and empower your viewers, your brand will become a trusted and respected presence on TikTok, enriching lives and fostering a sense of community in the process.

In the chapters that follow, we'll delve into strategies for measuring the success of your dental marketing efforts and sustaining your TikTok presence for the long term.

Chapter 7
Educating and Entertaining: Finding the Balance

"Balancing education and entertainment on TikTok is like the perfect dental check-up – informative and enjoyable."

In the world of TikTok marketing for dentists, striking the right balance between education and entertainment is key to keeping your audience engaged and informed. In this chapter, we'll explore how to find that equilibrium, creating content that both educates your viewers about oral health and entertains them, making your TikTok presence both valuable and enjoyable.

The Importance of Balance

Your TikTok content should educate your audience about oral health, dental procedures, and best practices. At the same time, it should be entertaining enough to captivate viewers' attention and encourage them to engage with your content. Achieving this balance can be a rewarding challenge.

Start with Education

- **Informative Explanations:** Begin with content that offers clear and informative explanations about dental topics. Explain procedures, oral hygiene practices, and the importance of regular dental check-ups in a straightforward and understandable manner.
- **Myth-Busting:** Address common misconceptions and myths about dentistry. Debunking myths can be both educational and engaging.
- **Tips and Tricks:** Share practical tips and tricks for maintaining oral health. These can include proper brushing and flossing techniques, advice on choosing the right toothbrush, or dietary recommendations for healthy teeth.

Case Studies: Showcase real-life case studies from your practice. Highlight patient transformations and success stories, providing a tangible demonstration of the benefits of dental care.

Entertain Along the Way

- **Storytelling:** Infuse storytelling elements into your content. Share anecdotes from your practice that illustrate important dental lessons. These stories can humanize your brand and connect with viewers emotionally.
- **Visual Creativity:** Leverage TikTok's creative tools and effects to make your videos visually engaging. Use animations, overlays, and transitions to enhance the entertainment value of your content.
- **Humor:** Appropriate humor can make dental content more entertaining. Share light-hearted anecdotes or amusing dental-related scenarios that your audience can relate to.
- **Interactive Challenges:** Create interactive challenges that educate while entertaining. For instance, challenge viewers to mimic proper brushing techniques in a fun and playful way.

Engage Your Audience

- **Ask Questions:** Encourage engagement by posing questions to your audience. Ask about their dental concerns, their oral hygiene routines, or their experiences with dental care. Respond to their comments and create a sense of dialogue.
- **Polls and Surveys:** Use TikTok's polling and survey features to gather feedback from your audience. You can ask them about the topics they'd like to see covered or their preferences for dental content.
- **Live Q&A Sessions:** Host live Q&A sessions where viewers can ask dental-related questions in real-time. These sessions provide immediate value and can be highly engaging.

Collaborate and Share

- **Collaborations:** Collaborate with other TikTok creators, especially those in the healthcare or dental niche. Joint videos can introduce your content to new audiences and provide diverse perspectives.
- **Patient Testimonials:** Share video testimonials from satisfied patients. These authentic stories can be highly engaging and reassuring for potential patients.
- **Behind-the-Scenes:** Offer glimpses into your dental practice's daily operations. Showcase your team's dedication, advanced technology, and commitment to patient care.

Analyze and Adapt

- **TikTok Analytics:** Continuously monitor TikTok's analytics to gain insights into how your educational and entertaining content performs. Identify which topics resonate most with your audience and adapt your strategy accordingly.

- **Audience Feedback:** Pay attention to audience feedback and comments. If viewers express a preference for certain types of content or have specific questions, consider incorporating their suggestions into your content plan.

- **Trends and Challenges:** Keep an eye on TikTok trends and challenges. When relevant, adapt these trends to your dental content, combining education with popular formats.

The Art of Timing

Timing is crucial when balancing education and entertainment. Consider the following:

- **Video Length:** TikTok videos are typically short, so make your points succinctly. Longer videos can be divided into a series to maintain engagement.
- **Hook Early:** Capture viewers' attention within the first few seconds of your video. This initial hook should pique their curiosity or offer a glimpse of what they'll learn or enjoy.
- **Visual Appeal:** Use visuals, graphics, and animations to enhance your content's visual appeal. Visual elements can convey information more effectively and keep viewers engaged.

Remain True to Your Brand

While balancing education and entertainment, always stay true to your brand identity. Your brand values, personality, and mission should shine through in every piece of content you create. This consistency helps build trust with your audience and reinforces your brand's credibility.

Balancing education and entertainment on TikTok is an art that requires practice and adaptability. By consistently delivering valuable educational content in an engaging and entertaining format, you can foster a loyal and informed audience while reinforcing your brand's reputation as a trusted source of dental knowledge.

In the chapters that follow, we'll delve into strategies for collaborations, going viral, and measuring the success of your dental marketing efforts on TikTok.

Chapter 8
Collaborations and Influencer Partnerships

"Influence isn't just about numbers; it's about making a lasting impact on smiles and lives."

Collaborations and influencer partnerships are powerful strategies for expanding your reach and credibility on TikTok. In this chapter, we'll explore how to leverage these opportunities effectively to enhance your dental marketing efforts and connect with a broader audience.

The Benefits of Collaborations

Collaborating with other TikTok creators or professionals in your industry can offer several advantages:

- **Reach a New Audience:** Partnering with others introduces your content to their followers, potentially expanding your reach exponentially.
- **Leverage Expertise:** Collaborating with dental experts or influencers allows you to tap into their knowledge and credibility, enhancing your content's authority.
- **Diverse Perspectives:** Collaborators bring diverse viewpoints and creativity to your content, making it more engaging and informative.
- **Cross-Promotion:** Mutual promotion helps both you and your collaborators gain more followers and engagement.

Choosing the Right Collaborators

Effective collaborations begin with selecting the right partners:

- **Relevance:** Collaborate with TikTok creators whose content aligns with dentistry or healthcare. Look for those who share your target audience.
- **Credibility:** Partner with influencers or professionals who have a credible and authentic online presence. Their endorsement can significantly impact your brand.
- **Engagement:** Examine their engagement metrics, such as likes, comments, and shares. Collaborators with an engaged following are more likely to help your content gain traction.
- **Values Alignment:** Ensure that your collaborators' values and messaging align with your brand. Consistency in messaging is essential for brand credibility.

Types of Collaborations

Collaborations can take various forms:

- **Joint Videos:** Create videos together on a shared topic or challenge. Both partners can post the same video on their accounts, tagging and mentioning each other.
- **Guest Appearances:** Feature each other in your respective videos. This can involve interviews, Q&A sessions, or simply appearing in each other's content.
- **Challenges:** Participate in or create joint challenges. Challenges often go viral and can garner significant attention.
- **Educational Series:** Collaborate on a series of educational videos, with each partner contributing their expertise to different topics.

Planning and Executing Collaborations

Successful collaborations require careful planning and execution:

- **Set Objectives:** Define clear objectives for the collaboration. Is it to reach a specific follower milestone, educate your audiences, or promote a particular dental service or product?
- **Content Planning:** Collaborate on content ideas and themes that align with both partners' expertise and interests.
- **Promotion:** Coordinate how you'll promote the collaboration. Decide on posting dates, captions, and hashtags.
- **Engagement:** Engage with each other's audiences by responding to comments and fostering dialogue.
- **Contractual Agreements:** In some cases, especially with influencer partnerships, you may need a formal agreement outlining roles, expectations, and compensation.

Building Relationships

Building relationships with collaborators is essential for long-term success:

- **Communicate:** Maintain open and transparent communication with your collaborators. Discuss ideas, feedback, and expectations.
- **Show Appreciation:** Express gratitude for their collaboration and the value they bring to your content.
- **Reciprocate:** Be willing to collaborate again in the future. Reciprocate their support by promoting their content and projects.

Influencer Partnerships

Influencer partnerships involve working with TikTok creators who have a substantial following and influence in your industry. Here's how to make the most of influencer partnerships:

- **Identify the Right Influencer:** Select influencers whose values, content, and audience align with your brand. Verify their credibility and engagement.

- **Negotiate Terms:** Discuss the terms of the partnership, including compensation, content expectations, and posting schedules.

- **Content Collaboration:** Work closely with the influencer to co-create content that seamlessly integrates your brand message.

- **Measuring Impact:** Use TikTok's analytics to assess the impact of the partnership. Track follower growth, engagement, and brand mentions.

- **Long-Term Relationships:** Consider building long-term relationships with influencers for ongoing collaboration and brand advocacy.

Ethical Considerations

Maintaining ethical standards in influencer partnerships is crucial:

- **Disclosure:** Ensure that influencers clearly disclose their relationship with your brand to maintain transparency and comply with advertising guidelines.
- **Authenticity:** Encourage influencers to provide honest reviews and opinions. Authenticity builds trust with their audience.
- **Legal Compliance:** Be aware of legal requirements related to influencer partnerships, including disclosure and endorsement guidelines.

Collaborations and influencer partnerships can be instrumental in expanding your TikTok presence as a dentist. When executed effectively and ethically, they can help you reach a wider audience, establish credibility, and foster long-term brand loyalty. In the chapters that follow, we'll explore strategies for maximizing your reach, measuring success, and overcoming common challenges in dental TikTok marketing.

Chapter 9
Going Viral: Strategies for Maximum Reach

"Going viral isn't luck; it's a mix of strategy, creativity, and connecting with the hearts of viewers."

Going viral on TikTok can catapult your dental marketing efforts to new heights, reaching an audience far beyond your current followers. In this chapter, we'll explore strategies to help your TikTok content go viral and achieve maximum reach.

Understand the Viral Algorithm

TikTok's algorithm plays a significant role in determining which videos go viral. Understanding how it works can help you tailor your content for maximum visibility:

- **Engagement:** TikTok prioritizes content that receives high engagement, such as likes, comments, and shares. Encourage viewers to interact with your videos.

- **Watch Time:** The longer viewers watch your videos, the better. Create compelling content that keeps viewers engaged until the end.

- **Consistency:** Posting regularly and maintaining a consistent schedule can signal to TikTok's algorithm that you're an active creator.

High-Quality Visuals and Sound

Visual and audio quality matter on TikTok. To go viral, ensure that:

- **Video Quality:** Record videos in high resolution to make them visually appealing.
- **Audio:** Use clear audio with minimal background noise. Consider adding music or voiceovers to enhance the viewer experience.

Leveraging Trends and Challenges

TikTok trends and challenges have the potential to catapult your content to viral status:

- **Participate Actively:** Join trending challenges and use popular hashtags to increase the discoverability of your content.
- **Put a Unique Spin:** While participating in trends, add your own unique twist that aligns with your dental expertise.
- **Create Your Own Challenges:** Launching your dental-related challenges can position you as a trendsetter and attract user-generated content.

Educational and Entertaining Content

The right balance of education and entertainment can capture viewers' attention and keep them engaged:

- **Informative Content:** Share valuable dental knowledge, tips, and insights. Make viewers feel like they're learning something important.
- **Entertaining Hooks:** Begin your videos with attention-grabbing hooks or stories to pique viewers' curiosity.
- **Visual Creativity:** Use TikTok's creative tools, like filters and effects, to make your content visually appealing.

Audience Engagement

Engagement is key to going viral:

- **Ask Questions:** Encourage viewers to comment, like, and share your content by asking questions or posing challenges.
- **Respond Actively:** Respond promptly to comments and engage with your audience. This interaction signals to TikTok's algorithm that your content is worth promoting.
- **Collaborations:** Collaborate with other TikTok creators, especially those with a substantial following. Their engagement can boost your content's visibility.

Consistent Posting Schedule

Consistency is vital for going viral:

- **Regular Posting:** Stick to a regular posting schedule to keep your audience engaged and coming back for more.
- **Variety of Content:** Offer a variety of content, including educational videos, behind-the-scenes glimpses, and trend-related content.
- **Quality Over Quantity:** While consistency is crucial, never compromise on the quality of your content. High-quality videos are more likely to go viral.

Optimizing Your Profile

Your TikTok profile plays a role in attracting new viewers:

- **Profile Picture:** Use a professional and recognizable profile picture, such as your clinic's logo or a clear photo of yourself.
- **Bio:** Craft an engaging and informative bio that clearly communicates your dental expertise and what viewers can expect from your content.
- **Link in Bio:** If applicable, include a link to your dental practice's website or booking page in your bio.

Collaboration with Influencers

Partnering with influencers can expand your reach:

- **Choose the Right Influencer:** Collaborate with influencers who align with your brand and target audience.
- **Co-create Content:** Work with influencers to co-create content that educates and entertains while leveraging their reach.
- **Promote Collaborations:** Both you and the influencer should promote the collaboration on your respective accounts.

Consistent Improvement

Monitor your content's performance and continuously improve:

- **TikTok Analytics:** Analyze TikTok's analytics to identify what works and what doesn't. Adjust your content strategy accordingly.
- **A/B Testing:** Experiment with different types of content, hooks, and formats to see what resonates best with your audience.
- **Stay Updated:** Keep up with TikTok trends, features, and changes to adapt your strategy as the platform evolves.

Encourage Sharing

Make it easy for viewers to share your content:

- **Share Buttons:** Use TikTok's share buttons to encourage viewers to send your videos to friends and family.
- **Call to Action (CTA):** Include a CTA in your video asking viewers to share it if they found it helpful or entertaining.
- **Collaborative Sharing:** Collaborate with others and ask them to share your content, especially during joint campaigns.

Going viral on TikTok is a combination of strategy, creativity, and a deep understanding of your audience. By consistently creating engaging and educational content, participating in trends, and actively engaging with your viewers, you increase your chances of achieving viral success. In the chapters that follow, we'll explore strategies for measuring success, overcoming challenges, and sustaining your TikTok presence for the long term.

Chapter 10
Measuring Success: Analytics and Insights

"The path to success on TikTok is paved with data-driven insights, revealing the smiles you've left in your wake."

In the dynamic world of TikTok marketing for dentists, measuring the success of your content and campaigns is crucial to refine your strategy and achieve your marketing goals. In this chapter, we'll delve into the essential aspects of analytics and insights on TikTok to help you make data-driven decisions and maximize your dental marketing efforts.

The Value of Analytics

TikTok provides a range of analytical tools and insights to help you assess the performance of your content and overall strategy. These insights empower you to:

- **Track Progress:** Monitor the growth of your TikTok account, including follower count and video views.

- **Audience Insights:** Understand your audience demographics, including age, gender, location, and interests.

- **Content Performance:** Analyze the performance of individual videos, measuring metrics like likes, comments, shares, and watch time.

- **Effectiveness of Hashtags:** Determine which hashtags drive the most engagement and visibility for your content.

- **Follower Growth:** Track how your collaborations and content impact your follower growth over time.

Key Metrics to Monitor

To measure the success of your dental marketing efforts on TikTok effectively, pay close attention to the following key metrics:

- **Follower Growth:** Analyze your follower count over time. A steady increase indicates that your content is resonating with your audience.

- **Video Views:** Monitor the number of views your videos receive. Higher view counts suggest increased reach and engagement.

- **Likes and Comments:** Engagement metrics like likes and comments are strong indicators of content quality and audience interest.

- **Shares:** The number of times your content is shared can amplify its reach and visibility.

- **Watch Time:** Track how long viewers watch your videos. Longer watch times indicate that your content is engaging and valuable.

- **Hashtag Performance:** Evaluate which hashtags are most effective in boosting your content's visibility and engagement.

Understanding Your Audience

To tailor your content and strategy effectively, gain insights into your TikTok audience:

- **Demographics:** Analyze the age, gender, and location of your followers. This information helps you create content that resonates with your specific audience.

- **Interest Insights:** Discover your audience's interests and preferences. Use this data to craft content that aligns with their tastes.

- **Peak Activity Times:** Identify when your audience is most active on TikTok. Posting during peak times can increase visibility.

Making Data-Driven Decisions

Armed with analytics and insights, you can make informed decisions to refine your dental marketing strategy:

- **Content Optimization:** Identify the type of content that performs best and create more of it. Tailor your content to address your audience's interests and concerns.

- **Hashtag Strategy:** Focus on hashtags that drive engagement and visibility. Experiment with trending and niche hashtags to expand your reach.

- **Posting Schedule:** Adjust your posting schedule to align with when your audience is most active.

- **Collaboration Selection:** Evaluate the impact of collaborations on your follower growth and engagement. Continue partnering with creators who deliver positive results.

- **Content Trends:** Stay updated on TikTok trends and adapt your content to leverage popular formats.

A/B Testing

Experimentation is key to understanding what works best on TikTok:

- **Content Variations:** Create multiple versions of a video with slight variations. Test different hooks, captions, or video lengths to identify what resonates most with your audience.

- **Posting Times:** Test different posting times and days to determine when your content receives the most engagement.

- **Hashtag Experiments:** Experiment with different sets of hashtags to gauge their impact on video performance.

Staying Ethical and Compliant

While analysing data and making data-driven decisions, ensure that you follow TikTok's guidelines and ethical standards:

- **Transparency:** Be transparent with your audience about data collection and usage in compliance with privacy regulations.

- **Ethical Use of Analytics:** Use data ethically and responsibly. Avoid spammy or misleading tactics to boost metrics artificially.

- **Compliance:** Adhere to TikTok's terms of service and community guidelines to maintain a positive and respectful presence on the platform.

Continuous Improvement

TikTok marketing is an ever-evolving field. Continuously analyze your analytics, stay updated on platform changes, and adapt your strategy accordingly to achieve ongoing success.

By harnessing the power of analytics and insights, you can refine your TikTok marketing efforts as a dentist, engage your audience effectively, and make data-driven decisions to enhance your presence on the platform. In the chapters that follow, we'll explore strategies for overcoming common challenges and sustaining your TikTok presence for the long term.

Chapter 11
Overcoming Challenges in Dental TikTok Marketing

"Challenges are the stepping stones to greater heights; in TikTok marketing, they lead to stronger connections."

While TikTok offers numerous opportunities for dental marketing, it also presents its fair share of challenges. In this chapter, we'll address these challenges and provide strategies to overcome them, allowing you to navigate the world of dental marketing on TikTok more effectively.

Challenge 1: Generating Content Ideas

Solution: Content ideation can be a challenge, but it's essential for a successful TikTok presence. Here are ways to generate fresh content ideas:

- **Patient Stories:** Share real-life patient success stories or transformations. These stories can be both educational and inspiring.
- **FAQs:** Answer common dental questions or concerns in short videos. Consider using the "duet" feature to compare popular myths with factual information.
- **Behind-the-Scenes:** Offer a glimpse into your dental practice's daily operations. Showcasing your team, technology, and commitment to patient care can be compelling.
- **Trending Challenges:** Participate in trending challenges and adapt them to dental themes.
- **Educational Series:** Create a series of educational videos that dive deep into specific dental topics, such as oral hygiene, orthodontics, or cosmetic dentistry.

- **Collaborations:** Collaborate with other TikTok creators, including fellow dentists or healthcare professionals, to bring diverse perspectives and content ideas.

Challenge 2: Building a Following

Solution: Growing your follower count can be challenging, but consistency and engagement are key:

- **Consistent Posting:** Stick to a regular posting schedule to keep your audience engaged and returning for more content.

- **Engage Actively:** Respond to comments, answer questions, and foster a sense of community with your audience.

- **Collaborations:** Partner with TikTok influencers or creators in your niche to tap into their follower base and gain exposure.

- **Cross-Promotion:** Promote your TikTok account on your other social media platforms, website, and in your dental practice.

Challenge 3: Balancing Education and Entertainment

Solution: Striking the right balance between educating and entertaining your audience is crucial. Here's how to manage this challenge:

- **Content Themes:** Plan your content around a mix of educational and entertaining themes. Alternate between informative videos and those with a more lighthearted or engaging approach.
- **Storytelling:** Incorporate storytelling elements into your educational content to make it more relatable and engaging.
- **Audience Feedback:** Pay attention to audience feedback and adapt your content based on their preferences and interests.

Challenge 4: Staying Up-to-Date with Trends

Solution: TikTok trends change rapidly, but staying informed is essential:

- **Dedicated Time:** Dedicate time each day to browse TikTok and stay updated on the latest trends and challenges.
- **Adaptation:** When you identify a relevant trend, adapt it to your dental content to keep it fresh and engaging.
- **Collaborate:** Collaborate with creators who are in touch with the latest trends to learn from their expertise.

Challenge 5: Maintaining Ethical Marketing Practices

Solution: Upholding ethical standards is crucial in dental TikTok marketing:

- **Transparency:** Clearly disclose any relationships, sponsorships, or affiliations in your content when promoting products or services.
- **Honesty:** Always provide accurate and truthful information in your content. Avoid exaggerations or misleading claims.
- **Respect for Privacy:** Respect patient privacy and obtain consent when sharing patient stories or before-and-after photos.

Challenge 6: Handling Negative Comments or Feedback

Solution: Negative comments are a common challenge, but how you respond is key:

- **Professionalism:** Respond professionally and respectfully to negative comments. Address concerns or misconceptions with accurate information.
- **Ignore Trolls:** Ignore or block users who engage in trolling or harassment. Do not engage in arguments or negativity.
- **Feedback Loop:** Use negative feedback constructively to improve your content and address any genuine issues.

Challenge 7: Adapting to Algorithm Changes

Solution: TikTok's algorithm evolves, impacting content visibility.

Here's how to adapt:

- **Monitor Changes:** Stay informed about TikTok's algorithm updates and adjust your strategy accordingly.
- **Consistency:** Maintaining a consistent posting schedule can signal to the algorithm that you're an active and engaged creator.
- **Engagement:** Encourage engagement on your videos through likes, comments, and shares to signal to the algorithm that your content is valuable.

Challenge 8
Legal and Regulatory Compliance
Solution: Adherence to legal and regulatory standards is paramount:

- **Consult Professionals:** Seek legal advice to ensure that your content and promotions comply with healthcare and advertising regulations.
- **Stay Informed:** Stay updated on evolving regulations in dental marketing and make necessary adjustments to your content and strategy.

By acknowledging and proactively addressing these challenges, you can navigate the world of dental TikTok marketing with greater confidence and success. Remember that persistence and a commitment to ethical practices are key to building a strong and enduring presence on the platform. In the chapters that follow, we'll explore strategies for sustaining your TikTok presence and integrating it with your overall marketing efforts.

Chapter 12
Avoiding Common Mistakes: Lessons Learned

"Mistakes are our greatest teachers; in TikTok marketing, they're the notes that lead to harmonious success."

In the world of TikTok marketing for dentists, avoiding common pitfalls and learning from mistakes is crucial for long-term success. In this chapter, we'll explore the most frequent mistakes made in dental TikTok marketing and share valuable lessons to help you steer clear of them.

Mistake 1: Lack of a Content Strategy

Lesson Learned: A well-defined content strategy is the backbone of successful TikTok marketing. Without it, you risk creating random and inconsistent content that may not resonate with your audience.

Solution: Create a content strategy that outlines your goals, target audience, content themes, posting schedule, and key performance indicators (KPIs). This strategy will serve as a roadmap for your TikTok journey, ensuring that your content is purposeful and aligned with your marketing objectives.

Mistake 2: Neglecting Audience Engagement

Lesson Learned: TikTok is a social platform, and engagement is paramount. Ignoring comments, failing to respond to questions, or neglecting audience interactions can lead to a disconnect with your viewers.

Solution: Actively engage with your audience by responding to comments, answering questions, and fostering a sense of community. Show that you value their feedback and appreciate their support.

Mistake 3: Overlooking Analytics

Lesson Learned: Neglecting to analyse your TikTok analytics means missing out on valuable insights that can inform your content strategy and growth efforts.

Solution: Regularly review your TikTok analytics. Track metrics like follower growth, video views, likes, and shares. Use these insights to identify what works and what doesn't, allowing you to refine your content and strategy over time.

Mistake 4: Focusing Solely on Promotion

Lesson Learned: Overly promotional content can turn off viewers. TikTok users are looking for authentic and engaging content rather than blatant advertising.

Solution: Balance your content mix. While it's important to promote your dental practice, also create educational, entertaining, and informative content. Building a genuine connection with your audience will yield better results in the long run.

Mistake 5: Ignoring TikTok Trends

Lesson Learned: TikTok is a trend-driven platform. Neglecting to incorporate relevant trends into your content can lead to decreased visibility and engagement.

Solution: Stay informed about TikTok trends and challenges. Adapt these trends to your dental content to keep your videos fresh and appealing to a wider audience.

Mistake 6: Neglecting Collaboration Opportunities

Lesson Learned: Failing to collaborate with other TikTok creators or influencers in your niche means missing out on valuable exposure and potential growth.

Solution: Seek collaboration opportunities with creators who share your target audience. Collaborations can introduce your content to new followers and provide diverse perspectives.

Mistake 7: Inconsistent Posting

Lesson Learned: Irregular posting can lead to decreased visibility and engagement. TikTok's algorithm favors consistent and active creators.

Solution: Establish a posting schedule and stick to it. Consistency signals to the algorithm that you're an engaged creator, increasing the likelihood of your content being promoted.

Mistake 8: Neglecting Educational Content

Lesson Learned: TikTok users appreciate informative content. Neglecting to educate your audience about dental health can limit your impact.

Solution: Create educational content that addresses common dental concerns, offers tips, and provides valuable insights. Balancing education with entertainment can capture and retain viewer interest.

Mistake 9: Lack of Authenticity

Lesson Learned: Authenticity is a cornerstone of successful TikTok marketing. Inauthentic or overly scripted content can deter viewers.

Solution: Be yourself in your videos. Share authentic stories, experiences, and insights from your dental practice. Authenticity builds trust and resonates with viewers.

Mistake 10: Failing to Stay Ethical

Lesson Learned: Ethical lapses, such as providing inaccurate information or promoting questionable products, can damage your reputation and credibility.

Solution: Uphold ethical standards in your TikTok marketing. Ensure that your content is truthful, transparent, and respectful of patient privacy. Always adhere to relevant healthcare and advertising regulations.

Mistake 11: Neglecting to Adapt

Lesson Learned: TikTok is a dynamic platform that evolves over time. Failing to adapt to changes in trends, algorithms, and audience preferences can hinder your growth.

Solution: Stay flexible and open to change. Continuously monitor TikTok's updates and trends and be willing to adjust your strategy accordingly.

Mistake 12: Not Learning from Feedback

Lesson Learned: Viewer feedback, including negative comments or constructive criticism, can provide valuable insights for improvement. Ignoring this feedback can limit your growth potential.

Solution: Embrace feedback as an opportunity for growth. Use it to refine your content, strategy, and approach. Engaging with constructive criticism demonstrates your commitment to improvement.

By learning from these common mistakes and applying the lessons provided, you can navigate the challenges of dental TikTok marketing with greater confidence and effectiveness. Building a strong and enduring presence on TikTok requires dedication, adaptability, and a commitment to ethical and authentic content. In the chapters that follow, we'll explore strategies for sustaining your TikTok presence and integrating it with your overall marketing efforts.

Chapter 13
Keeping Up with TikTok Trends

"In the ever-changing landscape of TikTok, staying relevant means dancing to the rhythm of trends."

TikTok is a platform that thrives on trends, challenges, and constant innovation. To stay relevant and successful in your dental TikTok marketing efforts, it's crucial to keep up with TikTok's ever-changing landscape. In this chapter, we'll explore strategies for staying in tune with TikTok trends and making the most of them for your dental marketing.

The Importance of TikTok Trends

TikTok trends are like currents in a river – they can carry your content to new heights or leave it stagnant.

Here's why staying current with TikTok trends matters:

Visibility: Trend-related content has a higher chance of appearing on users' For You Pages, increasing its visibility.

Engagement: Trends often generate higher engagement, such as likes, comments, and shares, as users enjoy participating in popular challenges.

Freshness: Trends keep your content fresh and exciting, making your profile more appealing to both current and potential followers.

Strategies for Staying Informed

To keep up with TikTok trends effectively, consider these strategies:

Daily Browsing: Dedicate time each day to scroll through TikTok. This helps you spot emerging trends and get a feel for what's popular.

Follow Trendsetters: Identify TikTok creators known for setting trends in your niche or industry. Follow and engage with their content to stay informed.

Explore the Discover Page: The "Discover" page often showcases trending content and challenges. Regularly check this section for inspiration.

Hashtags: Monitor trending hashtags on TikTok. Participating in or creating content around trending hashtags can boost your visibility.

Engage with Your Audience: Encourage your followers to suggest trends or challenges they'd like to see you participate in. Engaging with your audience can uncover unique trends.

Adapting Trends to Dentistry

TikTok trends are diverse, and not all may align with dental marketing. However, with creativity and adaptation, you can make most trends relevant to your content:

Educational Twist: Add an educational twist to trending challenges. For example, if there's a dance challenge, incorporate dental facts or tips into your video.

Behind-the-Scenes: Use trends as an opportunity to provide a behind-the-scenes look at your dental practice or the making of your content.

Before-and-After: Trends often involve transformations. Showcase dental transformations or smile makeovers as your take on a transformation trend.

Collaborations: Collaborate with fellow dentists or healthcare professionals to tackle trends together. This can add credibility and diversity to your content.

Content Originality

While trends are valuable, originality can set you apart on TikTok:

Put a Unique Spin: When participating in trends, add your own unique perspective or style. This can make your content stand out.

Create Original Challenges: Don't hesitate to start your dental-related challenges. If it catches on, you could start a trend yourself.

Incorporate Patient Stories: Share real patient success stories or testimonials, which can be both educational and engaging.

Trend Responsibly

While participating in trends, remember to do so responsibly:

Ethical Considerations: Ensure that your content, even when following trends, remains ethical, truthful, and respectful of patient privacy.

Age-Appropriate Content: Be mindful of the age group you're targeting and ensure that your content aligns with their interests and sensibilities.

Stay Authentic: Don't compromise your authenticity or professionalism to fit a trend. Your reputation as a dental professional should always take precedence.

Content Planning

Incorporating TikTok trends into your content strategy requires careful planning:

Timing: Participate in trends while they're still relevant. TikTok trends can be fleeting, so timely execution is key.

Relevance: Ensure that the trend aligns with your brand and message. It should make sense within the context of your dental marketing.

Frequency: Balance trend-related content with your regular content mix. Overloading your profile with trends can dilute your brand's identity.

By staying attuned to TikTok trends, adapting them creatively to your dental marketing, and ensuring responsible participation, you can leverage the platform's dynamic nature to your advantage. In the chapters that follow, we'll explore strategies for sustaining your TikTok presence and integrating it with your overall marketing efforts.

Chapter 14
Beyond TikTok: Integrating with Your Overall Marketing

"TikTok isn't just a platform; it's a thread woven into the tapestry of your holistic marketing strategy."

While TikTok offers a unique and powerful platform for dental marketing, your overall marketing strategy should be holistic and integrated. In this chapter, we'll explore strategies for seamlessly incorporating your TikTok efforts into your broader marketing plan for maximum impact.

TikTok as a Component of Your Marketing Mix

TikTok is just one piece of the marketing puzzle. To effectively integrate it into your overall strategy, consider these key principles:

Align with Brand Identity: Ensure that your TikTok content aligns with your overall brand identity and messaging. Consistency across all marketing channels is crucial for brand recognition.

Leverage Cross-Promotion: Promote your TikTok account on your website, other social media platforms, and in your dental practice. Encourage your existing audience to follow you on TikTok.

Coordinate Content: Your TikTok content should complement and reinforce your content on other platforms. For example, if you're running a dental awareness campaign on Instagram, create related TikTok content to cross-promote the message.

Integrating TikTok into Your Website

Your dental practice's website is a central hub for information. Integrate TikTok into your website effectively:

TikTok Widget: Add a TikTok widget to your website to display your latest TikTok videos or a curated selection. This encourages website visitors to explore your TikTok content.

Blog Content: Write blog posts that expand on the topics you cover in your TikTok videos. Embed TikTok videos within these posts to provide visual explanations and engage visitors.

Landing Pages: Create TikTok-specific landing pages on your website for campaigns or promotions featured on TikTok. This provides a seamless transition for interested viewers.

Email Marketing and TikTok

Leverage your email marketing strategy to promote your TikTok content:

Newsletter Inclusions: Include highlights of your recent TikTok content in your newsletters. Provide links to your TikTok profile or specific videos.

TikTok Challenges: Encourage email subscribers to participate in TikTok challenges or trends related to your dental practice. Share user-generated content in your newsletters.

Collaborations and Influencer Marketing

Collaborations with influencers can extend your reach beyond TikTok:

Cross-Promotion: Collaborate with TikTok influencers who align with your brand and values. They can promote your dental practice on their other social media platforms, creating a cross-channel effect.

Content Repurposing: Repurpose influencer-generated TikTok content for use on your other marketing channels, such as Instagram or YouTube.

Tracking and Measuring Impact

To measure the impact of your TikTok integration efforts:

UTM Parameters: Use UTM parameters to track the traffic generated from TikTok to your website. This allows you to understand how TikTok contributes to website visits and conversions.

Analytics Integration: Integrate TikTok analytics with your overall marketing analytics platform to get a comprehensive view of your marketing performance.

Consistency in Branding

Consistency in branding is essential across all channels:

Visual Branding: Ensure your visual branding elements, such as logos and color schemes, are consistent across TikTok, your website, and other social media platforms.

Tone and Messaging: Maintain a consistent tone and messaging style in your TikTok videos, blog posts, emails, and social media captions.

Adapting Content for Different Channels

While your TikTok content may serve as the foundation, adapt it to suit each marketing channel's unique characteristics:

Website: Create more in-depth content on your website, expanding on the topics introduced in TikTok videos.

Email: Craft email campaigns that use TikTok content as a starting point but offer additional value, such as exclusive offers or in-depth explanations.

Social Media: Tailor your TikTok content for other social media platforms. For example, create shorter clips for Instagram Stories or share behind-the-scenes footage on Facebook.

TikTok as a Customer Engagement Tool

Use TikTok to engage with your audience on a personal level:

Live Q&A: Host live Q&A sessions on TikTok, where viewers can ask dental questions or seek advice in real-time.

Patient Testimonials: Share patient testimonials or success stories on TikTok. These authentic stories can foster trust and engagement.

Interactive Content: Create polls, challenges, or interactive videos that encourage viewers to engage with your content and share their experiences.

Sustaining Your TikTok Presence

Maintaining a consistent presence on TikTok is essential for long-term success:

Content Calendar: Develop a content calendar that includes TikTok as a regular part of your marketing schedule.

Delegate Responsibility: Assign responsibility for TikTok content creation and management within your marketing team to ensure ongoing activity.

Regular Updates: Stay updated with TikTok trends and algorithm changes to adapt your strategy as needed.

By integrating TikTok seamlessly into your overall marketing strategy, you can maximize its impact, engage a broader audience, and build a cohesive brand presence across all marketing channels. In the final chapter, we'll summarize the key takeaways and provide a roadmap for your continued success in dental TikTok marketing.

Chapter 15
Sustaining Your TikTok Presence: Longevity in Dental Marketing

"Sustaining your TikTok presence is like a well-cared-for smile – it shines brighter with each passing day."

Sustaining your TikTok presence in the dynamic world of dental marketing requires dedication, adaptability, and a commitment to continuous improvement. In this final chapter, we'll explore strategies to ensure the long-term success of your dental TikTok marketing efforts.

Consistency is Key

Consistency is the cornerstone of a successful TikTok presence. To sustain your TikTok marketing efforts:

- **Content Calendar:** Maintain a content calendar that outlines your posting schedule. Consistency signals to the TikTok algorithm that you're an active creator.

- **Frequency:** Post regularly but maintain a balance. Quality should always take precedence over quantity.

- **Engagement:** Continue engaging with your audience by responding to comments and fostering a sense of community.

Evolving with TikTok Trends

TikTok is ever-evolving, and trends change rapidly. To stay relevant:

- **Daily Exploration:** Dedicate time each day to explore TikTok trends and challenges. Stay informed about what's popular.
- **Adaptation:** When you identify a relevant trend, adapt it creatively to your dental content to keep it fresh and engaging.
- **Originality:** While trends are essential, don't forget to inject your unique perspective and style into your content.

Measuring and Refining Your Strategy

Regularly measure the impact of your TikTok marketing:

- **Analytics:** Continue tracking key performance metrics like follower growth, video views, likes, and shares. Use these insights to refine your content and strategy.
- **Feedback Loop:** Embrace feedback as an opportunity for growth. Use constructive criticism to improve your content and approach.

Ethical and Responsible Marketing

Uphold ethical and responsible standards in your TikTok marketing:

- **Transparency:** Always be transparent with your audience about data collection and usage, and disclose any relationships or affiliations when promoting products or services.
- **Honesty:** Provide accurate and truthful information in your content. Avoid exaggerations or misleading claims.
- **Respect for Privacy:** Respect patient privacy and obtain consent when sharing patient stories or before-and-after photos.

Staying Informed

Stay informed about changes in TikTok's platform and policies:

- **TikTok Updates:** Keep up with TikTok's algorithm updates and policy changes. Adapt your strategy as needed to align with new developments.
- **TikTok Community:** Be an active part of the TikTok community. Engage with fellow creators, share experiences, and stay connected with the platform's evolving culture.

Long-Term Goals

Set long-term goals for your TikTok presence:

- **Brand Building:** Use TikTok as a tool to build and reinforce your dental practice's brand identity.
- **Education:** Continue to educate your audience about dental health and procedures. Become a trusted source of information.
- **Community:** Foster a loyal and engaged community of followers who turn to you for dental advice and support.

Integration with Overall Marketing

Integrate TikTok seamlessly into your overall marketing strategy:

- **Cross-Promotion:** Promote your TikTok account on your website, other social media platforms, and in your dental practice.
- **Content Alignment:** Ensure that your TikTok content aligns with your brand identity and messaging across all marketing channels.
- **Content Adaptation:** Adapt TikTok content for your website, email marketing, and other social media platforms to create a cohesive brand presence.

Future-Proofing Your Strategy

TikTok marketing is an ever-evolving field. To future-proof your strategy:

- **Adaptability:** Stay flexible and open to change. Be willing to adjust your strategy as TikTok and your audience evolve.

- **Experimentation:** Continue experimenting with new content formats, trends, and engagement strategies to keep your TikTok presence fresh and engaging.

- **Learning:** Stay curious and committed to learning. Attend webinars, read industry articles, and seek inspiration from other creators.

Celebrating Milestones

As you sustain your TikTok presence, celebrate milestones:

- **Follower Milestones:** Acknowledge and celebrate follower milestones, such as reaching 10,000 or 100,000 followers.
- **Content Achievements:** Recognize successful videos and content that receive a high level of engagement or go viral.
- **Impactful Stories:** Share stories of how your TikTok content positively impacted your audience or dental patients.

By following these strategies and maintaining a long-term perspective, you can sustain and grow your TikTok presence in the realm of dental marketing. Remember that TikTok success is a journey, and with dedication and a commitment to ethical and engaging content, you can continue to make a positive impact on your audience and dental practice.

Navigating TikTok's Dynamic Waters in Dental Marketing

As we conclude our journey through the world of TikTok marketing for dentists, I hope this book has provided you with valuable insights, strategies, and inspiration to excel in this dynamic and ever-evolving field. TikTok, with its immense reach and engagement potential, offers a unique opportunity for dental professionals to connect with their audience in new and meaningful ways.

Throughout this book, we've explored the power of TikTok marketing, from understanding your dental audience to crafting compelling content, navigating TikTok's features, leveraging hashtags and trends, and building your TikTok brand. We've delved into the intricacies of educating and entertaining your viewers, forging collaborations and influencer partnerships, and going viral with effective strategies.

We've also addressed common challenges and provided valuable lessons to help you avoid pitfalls in dental TikTok marketing. From content strategy and audience engagement to ethical marketing practices and adaptation to trends, you've gained a comprehensive understanding of how to navigate the TikTok landscape effectively.

Moreover, we've emphasised the importance of integrating TikTok into your overall marketing strategy. TikTok can be a powerful component of your marketing mix, provided it aligns with your brand identity, is promoted across various channels, and is integrated seamlessly into your website, email marketing, and collaborations with influencers.

Sustaining your TikTok presence for the long term requires dedication, adaptability, and ethical responsibility. Consistency, staying informed about trends and changes, and measuring your impact are vital components of a successful TikTok strategy. Remember, TikTok marketing is not just about short-term gains but building a lasting connection with your audience and strengthening your dental practice's brand.

As you continue your journey in dental TikTok marketing, don't forget to celebrate milestones along the way – from follower achievements to impactful stories of how your content positively influenced your audience and dental patients. Your dedication to this dynamic platform can lead to meaningful connections, educational impact, and business growth.

I encourage you to keep learning, experimenting, and adapting to the ever-changing TikTok landscape. Stay true to your brand, remain committed to ethical and responsible marketing practices, and always strive for authenticity in your content. By doing so, you can create a lasting impact on TikTok and in the world of dental marketing. Thank you for joining me on this TikTok marketing adventure. I wish you every success in your continued journey as a dental professional making waves on TikTok's dynamic waters. Here's to your continued growth and impact in the world of dental marketing!

www.ingramcontent.com/pod-product-compliance
Lightning Source LLC
Chambersburg PA
CBHW072255270326
41930CB00010B/2388